AARON KOENIG

FREAKI

I0068293

CRISIS
PROOF

The Handbook of
Financial Freedom

PR1V4T3
K3Y

AARON KOENIG

FREAKIN'
CRISIS
PROOF

The Handbook of
Financial Freedom

PR1V4T3
K3Y

Imprint

Aaron Koenig:
FREAKIN' CRISIS PROOF
The Handbook of Financial Freedom

Private Key Publishing
A division of Lamboluna LLC
2880 W Oakland Park Boulevard, Suite 225C
Oakland Park, 33311, Miami (FL)
Translation from German: Adrian Sanders
Graphic design: Jordi Palau
Cover Photo: Gabriel Barranco
ISBN: 978-0-578-77361-2

To my international readers:
This book might look quite German to you. All my experts, all economists I quote and most of the examples I use are from the German speaking world. I wrote this book originally in German for a German publisher and of course I know the country where I grew up the best, although I do not live there anymore. But I am sure that the insights you can win through this book can be useful everywhere on this small planet.

Contents

Preface by Rodolfo Andragnes   5

Introduction   9

1. Is a Crash Inevitable?   12
    1.1. The Euro, a Misconstruction   13
    1.2 The Fiat Money System   17
    1.3 The End of the China Boom   27
    1.4 A Vicious Circle   31

2. Digital Cash   44
    2.1. The Basics of Digital Money   45
    2.2 How to Use Bitcoin   54
    2.3 How to Fill Your Bitcoin Wallet   61
    2.4 Storing Bitcoin Securely   65

3. Is Bitcoin Crisis-Proof?   73
    3.1 Why Does Bitcoin Have Value?   74
    3.2 The World's Hardest Money   77
    3.3 Bitcoin Cannot be Stopped   80
    3.4 Bitcoin Works Without Banks   82
    3.5 Weaknesses of Bitcoin   84
    3.6 Stable Coins   89

4. Austrian Investing   95
    4.1 The Austrian School of Economics   96
    4.2 Mises' Theory of Money   98
    4.3 The Austrian Portfolio   102
    4.4 Weaknesses of Austrian Investing   110

5. Get Out of Tax Hell   113

    5.1 Reasons to Emigrate   115

    5.2 The Flag Theory   118

    5.3 Models of Taxation   121

    5.4 From Panama to Prospera   125

    5.5 But Who Would Build the Roads?   136

6. Mastering the Crisis   140

    5.1 Protect Your Privacy!   142

    5.2 Be Prepared For an Emergency!   148

    5.3 Protect Yourself From Crime!   153

    5.4 Strengthen Your Social Network!   155

7. Financially Free in Mind   157

    5.1 Mind Your Mind   158

    5.2 The Life Concept Ikigai   160

    5.3 Millionaire's Mind by T. Harv Eker   162

    5.4 Wealthy Mind by Tim and Kris Hallbom   165

    5.5 The Diamond Cutter Training by Geshe   170
        Michael Roach

8. Imagine   177

Aknowledgements   186

Comments   187

Images   193

Preface

by Rodolfo Andragnes

Rodolfo Andragnes is the co-founder of Bitcoin Argentina and the main organiser of the Latin American Bitcoin Conference (Labitconf).

In the 43 years I have lived as an Argentinian citizen, several zeros were removed from our currency to adjust it to skyrocketing inflation rates three times. Each time it also got a new name, it changed from *Peso Argentino* to *Austral* to *Peso Convertible* to simply *Peso*. I have also seen the appearance and decline of local currencies called *Patacones*, which were issued in certain provinces but supressed by the central government. I have seen us stumble over the same stones again and again, which forced many of my familiy members and friends to leave the country. And a new economic crisis seems inevitable.

Whilst some would say inflation is only a symptom of the structural disease of my country, it is a recurring formula used by many governments, because it is such an easy and tempting method for them. But it is a dangerous one, as inflation undermines the long term value that any society can create.

This is not only true for Argentina, it seems to be the standard in many Latin American countries, which are also plagued by a high level of corruption. Although in the Northern Hemisphere things seem to be a bit better, the Coronavirus panic has shown that governments everywhere are printing large amounts of money as a remedy to their problems.

Inflation, the Worst Remedy

For more than half a century, government money has no longer been backed by gold. Since the end of the Bretton Woods system in 1971, governments have been able to create money out of thin air without having to underly it with a real asset such as gold. They are using the unlimited tool of money creation to pay for their expenses and their gigantic projects, and they have been abusing it for their own benefit. Inflation is good for governments, as the debt they have piled up loses its value. But it is bad for normal taxpayers and savers, who are forced to use the money issued by the government and its central bank.

"Legal tender" is imposed by law as money that everyone has to accept as payment. In contrast, real money such as gold or silver is voluntarily accepted as a medium of exchange. It also fulfills the functions of being a unit of account and a store of value without any government having to enforce this.

One may think that we are free to choose the money we use, but governments do everything they can to prevent us from doing so. They make it illegal to use alternative currencies and put their creators in jail. This happened in the USA with the creator of the gold backed Liberty Dollar, Bernhard von Nothaus. Even the private posession of gold became illegal in the USA in 1933, by an executive order which was only repealed in 1974. In Argentina, governments often apply currency controls to prevent us from sending money out of the country. They also limit the amount of US dollars we are allowed to buy, which is why a vast black market for the US currency exists in my country (known as the *Blue Market* because we prefer the colour of our national flag).

The Freedom that Bitcoin Provides

In 2008 a new form of money was born: Bitcoin. Its qualities even surpass those of gold in terms of scarcity, portability, divisibility and non-counterfeitability. Furthermore, it can travel through the Internet at high speed, without any government being able to stop it or to "freeze an account". As Bitcoin is nothing but software, it is also programmable, which brings many advantages in usability and security.

Although Bitcoin is not physical, it has three characteristics that we thought only physical assets could provide:
- No two Bitcoins can be equal
- Bitcoins can be transfered without any intermediaries
- A Bitcoin belongs to the bearer without the need to disclose his identity.

This new monetary system is the most liberating model to date, because of its resilience to censorship, to forgery and to manipulation. Bitcoin is an asset which offers absolute certainty on its scarcity. It makes storage and usage more efficient. In my opinion, Bitcoin is a new opportunity for a society to become free. It allows us to abolish the evils that come with a government monopoly of the monetary system once and for all.

In Argentina we have been through many crises, from hyperinflation to frozen bank accounts. That's why Argentinians are more eagerly embracing Bitcoin than people in other, less crisis-struck countries. You don't have to convince us not to trust the banks or the government. We know that only too well. Unfortunately, in the times of our worst crises, Bitcoin was not yet available, but in the upcoming crisis we can use it to defend our financial freedom. And you can use it too. This book shows you how.

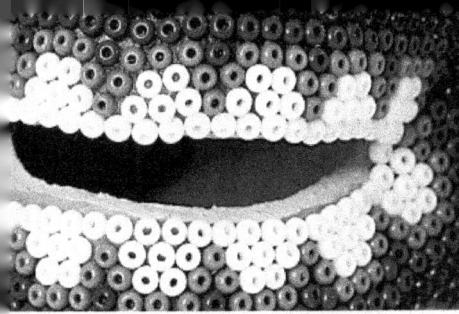

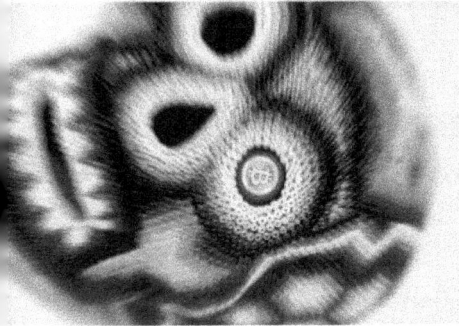

Introduction

Are we facing the biggest financial crisis ever? Will our debt-based monetary system finally collapse? Will we have to wait in queues in front of ATMs to get some cash, fearing that it will have lost most of its value?

It seems to be only a matter of time before the big crisis comes. Perhaps we are already in the middle of it when you read this book. But you can arm yourself against it. That is what this book is about. It gives tips on how to maintain your financial freedom despite negative interest rates, hyperinflation and capital controls.

Cryptocurrencies such as Bitcoin play an important role in this. They are designed in such a way that they cannot be manipulated by any central authority. No power in the world can stop a Bitcoin transfer or freeze a crypto account. Cryptocurrencies are extremely effective tools to secure our savings and to continue trading with each other when the banking system collapses.

In the short term, the price of Bitcoin can also fall if people panic. This could be observed at the beginning of the Corona crisis in March 2020, when the Bitcoin price, just like stocks and other securities, suddenly plunged sharply. When the central banks announced that they were pumping large amounts of money into the market, Bitcoin quickly rose again. Bitcoin is not yet a "safe haven" for investors; it is too new and unknown for that. But cryptocurrencies have so many advantages over the conventional financial system that they will prevail in the long run.

So far I have written three books on cryptocurrencies. In *A Beginners' Guide to Bitcoin and Austrian Economics* I explain why a free competition of currencies is superior to the current monetary system. *Cryptocoins – Investing in Digital Currencies* gives an overview of the different types of cryptocurrencies and provides many practical tips on how to deal with them. *The Decentralised Revolution* sheds light on the economic and political consequences that Bitcoin and Blockchain technology may have.

Cryptocurrencies also play a role in this book, but I look at them from a different perspective. In Chapter 2 I give a general introduction; in Chapter 3 I focus on the questions: How can Bitcoin help you secure your savings despite financial repression? How can you move your assets out of a country if necessary?

However, this book is not only about cryptocurrencies, but also about many other methods to defend your financial and individual freedom. For this I have worked with experts who are among the best in their fields. You can learn from Steffen Krug how to invest your money according to the findings of the Austrian School of Economics (Chapter 4). Christoph Heuermann knows where it is best to locate yourself and your company while paying as little tax as possible (Chapter 5). Security expert Bettina Falck gives tips on how to protect your life, health and property and how to survive a crisis (Chapter 6).

In Chapter 7, we take the topic of financial freedom a little further. Here we have a look at your attitude towards money, wealth and success in general. For this purpose I have explored some popular training methods that may bring you closer to financial freedom, namely *Millionaire's Mind* by T. Harv Eker, *Wealthy Mind* by Tim and Kris Hallbom and the *Diamond Cutter System* by Geshe Michael Roach. Chapter 8 is a very optimistic utopia of what a better world could look like after the great crisis.

The result is a practical handbook that enables you to live freely even in dire straits.

1. Is a Crash Inevitable?

Crash prophecies are booming. *The Biggest Crash Ever*[1], *World System Crash*[2], *The World Before the Greatest Economic Crisis of All Times*[3] – these are just a few of the books that have come out recently, triggering fear and anxiety. Also, on the Internet many authors warn of an unprecedented financial crisis. And even the research department of Deutsche Bank speculates, in its magazine *Konzept*, on the end of the current monetary system.[4] Is this just panic mongering? As we know, panic sells well. One could easily dismiss it as such. But unfortunately, there are many signs that the crisis prophets should be taken seriously. In this chapter we want to take a look at the deeper causes that could lead to a major financial and economic crisis.

1.1 The Euro, a Misconstruction

The Euro is a purely political construct. From an economic point of view, it makes no sense to force economies as different as the ones of Germany or Greece under one state currency monopoly. Some politicians wanted to push through the Euro in order to realise their vision of a "United States of Europe", others intended to end the monetary dominance of the Germans and their *Bundesbank*. Both went utterly wrong.

Export Boom and Target-2

The German export industry has benefited greatly from the fact that the external value of the euro is actually too weak for it. It can thus offer its goods more cheaply than in the days of the Deutsche Mark. The Italian lira and

Target-2-Balances (bn €)

Germany

Euro Crisis Monitor
Institute of Empirical Economic Research
Osnabrück University
Data source: European Central Bank

ECB	Austria	Belgium	Cyprus	Germany	Estonie	Spain
Finland	France	Greece	Ireland	Italy	Lithuania	Luxembourg
Latvia	Malta	Netherlands	Portugal	Slovenia	Slovakia	Out-NCBs

the French franc have been devalued several times in the past to compensate for the export strength of the German economy. This is no longer possible with the euro. However, the central banks of the other euro countries are now indebted to the German Bundesbank for nearly one trillion Euros via the so-called *Target 2* system. This was originally intended to settle short-term payment, not as a long-term overdraft loan to finance the export of German cars and machinery. It is foreseeable that this system will collapse sooner or later and the resulting losses will have to be borne by the German taxpayers.

Debt Without Borders

Since the introduction of the Euro, governments such as those of Greece or Italy, which are living particularly well above their means, can take on debt at much lower interest rates than they could at the time of the drachma or lira. Public debt has therefore risen sharply in almost all Eurozone countries. The originally agreed rules on Euro stability are being disregarded. Hardly any government

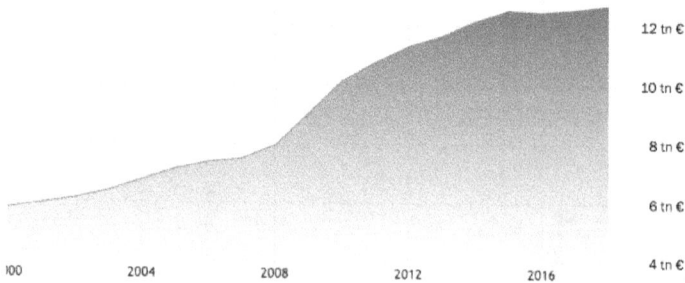

Rising Government Debt in the Euro Zone

still adheres to the debt limit of 60 per cent of gross national product, which was actually agreed upon. Through the *European Stability Mechanism (ESM)*, the Euro states are jointly liable for each other's debts, which was expressly forbidden in the Maastricht Treaty. Any company that did as badly as the Eurozone governments would have had to file for insolvency already.

The Fate of Monetary Unions

As a result of the ongoing Euro crisis, the European Union is further away than ever from the utopia (or dystopia?) of the "United States of Europe". The numerous problems of the single currency have led to much controversy. In weaker economies such as Greece or Portugal, many people feel that the governments of economically stronger countries are bullying them and restricting their sovereignty. Germans, Dutch or Austrians, for their part, do not see why they should pay for the misconduct of others with their taxes.

There is no European solidarity or even a "European patriotism". Instead, nationalist parties are gaining ground all over Europe, which is particularly evident in the elections to the powerless EU sham parliament. It is no wonder that the British despise the undemocratic Brussels central government and have left the EU. They will certainly not be the last. EU members like Poland, Hungary, Czechia or

Denmark, who have kept their national currencies, may not yet be ready to leave the EU, but they will certainly not give up their currencies for the Euro.

There has never been a successful example of a supra-national monetary union in history. The Latin Monetary Union between France, Belgium, Italy, Switzerland and later Greece existed from 1865 to 1926 but failed because of the different economic developments of the member states. The Scandinavian Coinage Union, which had been concluded between Sweden, Norway and Denmark since 1873, was also short-lived and disbanded in 1914.

Back to National Currencies?

I see no reason why the Euro should take a different course. Maybe Angela Merkel will "save" the Euro for a few more years with German taxpayers' money, which would only make the crash more expensive. But perhaps it will happen faster than we think. It is hard to imagine the consequences of a collapse of the Euro system. The debts of the Euro states are far too high to ever pay them back. The best way out from the governments' point of view would be a currency reform, but this would mean a signif-icant devaluation of all savings held in euros. You should therefore never invest your money in euros, as there is a high probability that at least part of it will be lost.

The monetary unions of the 19th and early 20th centuries were still based on a gold standard, but the Euro is a purely virtual currency, which is not backed by anything. A return to national money monopolies such as the D-Mark, which some nationalist politicians demand, is therefore not a sustainable solution, because the D-Mark was also unbacked monopoly money. While an artificial construct such as the Euro leads to particularly severe economic distortions compared with national currencies, the basic evil lies much deeper: it is the monetary system based on a state monopoly.

1.2 The Fiat Money System

Many people believe that the production of money is a genuine task of the state, but this is a myth. On the contrary, letting the state rule over money is a very bad idea. The ruling elites will always exploit their monopoly over money to their own interest, which very rarely coincides with the interests of the ordinary citizens. Monopolies are only ever good for those who hold them but harmful to everyone else. The state monopoly on money is no exception. Throughout history it has led to economic crises, hyperinflation, loss of savings and social upheaval.

Money is a Product of the Market

Money is not an invention of the state. It arose on the free market from the need of people for a general medium of exchange. You can see this well in informal economies, for example among the inmates of prisons, where cigarettes, canned fish or other scarce goods take on a monetary function. This happens voluntarily, not because the prison administration decides it.[5] In occupied Germany between the end of World War II and the currency reform of 1948, American cigarettes such as Marlboro or Lucky Strike functioned as currency, which was by no means planned by the occupying powers.

Cigarettes are of course not the perfect money; they are too easily smoked away or soaked by the rain. Also other goods like cattle, salt, shells or arrowheads, which have been used as money over the course of time, show various disadvantages. Independently of each other, people all over the world have come to use precious metals such as gold or silver as money because they have the qualities of good money. Precious metals are:

- scarce
- durable
- divisible
- fungible
- identifiable
- mintable
- easily transportable
- hard to falsify

From the Gold Standard to Bretton Woods

For thousands of years, gold and silver have therefore served as money. They still do as reserves of the central banks. In the 19th century, all major currencies were pegged to each other via the gold standard, which facilitated world trade and, combined with the industrial revolution, led to an unprecedented economic upswing. But at the outbreak of the First World War, governments abandoned the gold standard, as the war would not have been affordable with gold-backed currencies. After 1918, the financing of the war through debt money led to massive hyperinflation, particularly in Germany and Austria.

From 1944 until the early 1970s, there was still a kind of indirect gold standard. The US dollar, the world's anchor currency, was backed by gold, and all other major currencies had a fixed exchange ratio to the dollar. Unlike a genuine gold standard however, not all citizens but only the central banks had the right to exchange dollars for gold at the US Federal Reserve. This international monetary system, agreed in the Bretton Woods Agreement of 1944, worked quite well for some time. But when in the 1960s the US printed more and more dollars to finance the Vietnam War and some costly social reforms, many central banks distrusted the stability of the US dollar. They exercised their right to exchange their dollars for gold, which made the USA run out of gold reserves.

On 15. August 1971, President Nixon unilaterally terminated the Bretton Woods Agreement by ending the exchange of US dollars for gold. Since then, the world's currencies are no longer backed by precious metals. The monetary system which dominates the world since the 1971 is known as the Fiat Money system, from the Latin *fiat* = "let there be". This means that money is generated arbitrarily and not backed by any commodity.

Money Out of Thin Air

In today's financial system, money is created in several ways. On the one hand, by the central banks, which have the exclusive right to print banknotes and mint coins. They can also grant loans to the commercial banks for an interest from which all other interest rates are derived. However, a large part of the money supply is not created by the central banks, but by commercial banks every time they grant a loan. In the case of the Euro, they only have to keep 1% of it as a reserve at the central bank. They can create the remaining 99% virtually from scratch. This newly created money is credited to the borrower and booked by the bank as a receivable. New items are created on both sides of the balance sheet, thus increasing the money supply.

Unlike banks, however, citizens or business owners cannot pay off debts by such a "magic act" of money creation. They usually have to work hard for it and, for example, provide a lien on the house they mortgage for collateral. If they can no longer service the loan, the bank becomes the owner of the house that was bought with money created out of thin air. Does such a system also sound absurd and unfair to you?

To Whom Belongs Your Money?

Few people know that the money in "their" bank account is no longer their property, but merely a claim on the bank. From the bank's point of view it is a liability, which means that the bank promises to pay back the money. But how much this promise is worth is known to every Greek who stood in front of closed bank branches during the heyday of the Euro crisis and could no longer get hold of "his" money. At the time of the *Corralito* in Argentina in 2001, people's bank deposits were even blocked for almost a year and then devalued by nearly 50%.

The reason for those repressive measures is the so-called fractional reserve system. Banks do not have the full amount of money they owe their customers at their disposal. They actually keep only a small part – the fractional reserve – in their vaults. If more bank customers than usual were to withdraw their money at the same time, the banks would go bankrupt immediately. Especially in times of crisis there have been several bank runs. Many economic crises have started like that. Central banks were founded in the first place to avoid this. In times of crisis they are supposed to be the "Lender of Last Resort". But this is just the pretext for the existence of central banks. In reality, they were founded to finance wars. Central banks and a centralised monetary are benefitial for the ruling elite, but they have severe disadvantages for normal citizens.

The Cantillon Effect

The economist Richard Cantillon observed that in a monopoly money system, those who are close to the source of money benefit at the expense of all others. Cantillon himself was a beneficiary of one of the first central banking systems created by Scottish banker John Law for the King of France, which collapsed in 1720 to the detriment of many small investors. Therefore he knew from his own experience what he was researching.

According to Cantillon, in a Fiat money system the first recipients of money are the winners: they can use the newly created money to buy goods at prices that have not yet changed. After the new money is passed from hand to hand, the prices of goods rise because their quantities do not grow at the same rate as the money supply. Consequently, the later recipients of the new money are the disadvantaged. They can only buy the goods at the new, higher prices.

This so-called *Cantillon Effect* leads to a redistribution of wealth from workers and pensioners to the ones close to central power. The profiteers are an ever growing state apparatus and the financial industry which is closely intertwined with it. The Cantillon Effect is a central cause of the widening gap between rich and poor. If Karl Marx had understood more of economics, he would have realised that the centralisation of money production in the hands of the state as called for in the Communist Manifesto[6], must lead to growing injustice. It is grotesque that the Marxist model of a state central bank has prevailed nearly everywhere today, even in the supposedly "capitalist" states, although it is in obvious contradiction to the principles of a free market economy.

The Hidden Tax of Inflation

Today's state-controlled currencies do not have all the characteristics of good money described above. Their greatest weakness is that they are not scarce and can be multiplied

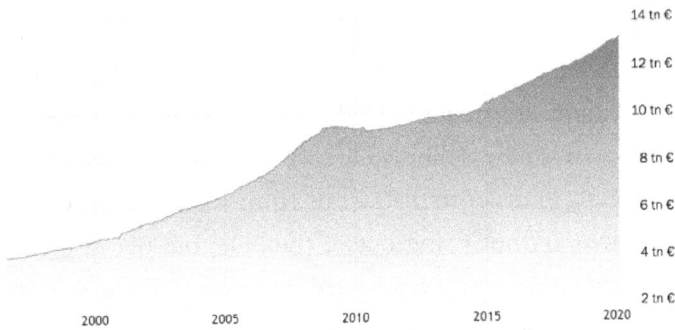

Rising Money Supply of the Euro Zone

25

at will by central and commercial banks. Through the increase of the money supply, also called inflation (from Latin *inflare* = to blow up), money inevitably loses purchasing power. The amount of goods and services do not grow to the same extent as the money supply, so prices need to rise. For those in power, increasing the money supply is a tempting way of financing "social benefits" in order to make themselves popular with voters and thus ensure their re-election. Inflation is a hidden tax, not as unpopular as a regular one, which must be approved by parliament.

Many people, even economists, use the word *inflation* when they talk about a rise of prices. But these are two different things. They are closely linked but should be clearly distinguished. The inflation of the money supply is the main reason why prices are rising. Without it, they should fall due to increased productivity and a better global division of labour. This is still the case with some goods such as computers and mobile phones, even despite inflation.

When the news speaks of inflation, they are actually referring to the price of a basket of goods, which is arbitrarily defined by the government. However, things like stocks or real estate, whose prices rise particularly strongly due to inflation, are not included in this basket at all. Here, the powerful elite deliberately mix up terms and use them incorrectly in order to distract us from what is really going on. Prices are not rising out of the blue, but because governments and central banks are manipulating the money supply. I therefore recommend to use the term inflation only in its literal meaning, which is the increase of the money supply, and otherwise to speak of a rise of prices. It is important that we do not confuse cause and effect.

The prevailing monetary system is unfair and harmful. It leads to economic distortions at the expense of the working population. Since it came into existence in its pure form in 1971, public and private debt have exploded in all major economies. It is completely impossible to ever repay this debt in an honest fashion. The only solutions from the governments' point of view are debt cuts, hyperinflation or currency reforms – or a combination of these. In all cases, citizens' financial savings will be severely devalued or even completely destroyed. The collapse of our monetary system is still delayed by printing more and more money, but this sick system will not last very much longer.

A Better Monetary System

But what is the alternative? Ludwig von Mises, probably the most outstanding economist of the 20th century, has proposed a return to the gold standard and the end of the fractional reserve system. Every banknote would then be nothing more than a receipt for gold stored in a bank. Such a full backing of money would require governments to be much more disciplined than they are today because gold cannot be multiplied at will like paper or digital money. Excessive national debt and chronic inflation, which are commonplace today, would be ruled out. Under a gold standard, wars would hardly be financeable.

But will governments voluntarily give away control of the monetary system? I doubt it. All major governments would have to agree on a new gold standard, which is extremely unlikely. If we want a better monetary system, we can only do it without governments. The Austrian economist and Nobel Prize winner Friedrich August von Hayek therefore proposed the separation of money and state and free competition between currencies as a solution as early as 1976.

"The only way to save civilisation in the end will be to remove governments' power over money," writes Hayek in his book *The Denationalisation of Money*. "The instability of the market economy to date is a consequence of the fact that the most important regulator of the market mechanism, money, has itself been excluded from regulation by the market process."[7]

In 1976 Hayek's proposal seemed utopian, but today it has become a reality thanks to cryptocurrencies such as Bitcoin. And perhaps Ludwig von Mises' wish will come true in the form of a gold-backed, decentralised cryptocoin. We will have a closer look at this in Chapters 2 and 3.

Boomtown Shanghai

1.3 The End of the China Boom

China has undergone an astonishing economic development in recent decades. From a communist poorhouse, where millions of people starved to death, it has risen to become an economic superpower due to the reforms introduced by Deng Xiaoping since the late 1970s. This was possible because the communist government has allowed much more market economy and private enterprise.

For many years, the Chinese economy grew at rates between 10 and 15% per year. Western companies have benefited greatly from China's increasing prosperity. More than a billion Chinese have been able to afford more goods, from German cars to Italian fashion items. Without the

29

development of the huge Chinese market the continued export success of several Western countries would probably not have been possible.

Growth by Debt

But there are signs that this boom, which has lasted for decades, is gradually – or perhaps abruptly – coming to an end. Much of China's growth is financed by cheap credit. If you borrow money for 4% and invest it in Chinese real estate, which has been rising by 20% every year, the calculation is simple. Even if the property remains unrented and generates no income, as long as you can sell it at a profit after one year, the deal is worthwhile. But what happens if growth rates flatten out, which has been the case recently? What happens if interest rates are raised? Then the

Ghost Town Kangbashi

game no longer pays off, investors withdraw their money and the house of cards collapses. Although only a small proportion of Chinese debt comes from abroad, if the US Federal Reserve raises its interest rates, the Chinese economy will be hit hard. Chinese analyst Niu Dau says: "China is the biggest bubble in the history of the world economy, and rising US interest rates will cause it to burst."[8]

Wasteful Planned Economy

As impressive as the Chinese economic miracle may be, China's economy is highly vulnerable. Many Chinese companies make operating losses and survive only because they repeatedly receive low-interest loans from the banks, at the behest of the government, which is not too keen on company bankruptcies. Although China has become much more market-oriented in recent years than it used to be, five-year plans and state intervention in the economy still exist. If the Chinese Communist Party decides that more growth should be generated not only in the south-east of the country but also in the poor north, then large cities will be built from scratch for billions of yuans. For example, the city of Kangbashi has been built on the border with Mongolia for around one million people. But hardly anyone wants to live there. The city is largely empty — a gigantic waste of resources that would be impossible in a market economy.[9]

The Japanese Bubble

History does not repeat itself, but it often rhymes. A look at Japan shows what China could be facing. In the 1980s, Japan was considered to become the leading economic power, with Japanese companies taking more and more market share from their competitors in the USA and Europe. The Empire of the Rising Sun experienced a meteoric rise of stock market and real estate prices. In the mid-1980s, Japanese real estate was several times more expensive than comparable US real estate. At the peak of the boom, the area of the Imperial Palace in Tokyo alone had a higher market value than the entire state of California. But unfortunately, Japanese growth was based on low interest rates and easy credit.

At the end of the 1980s, the US Federal Reserve raised its interest rates several times and the rapid growth of the Japanese economy slowed down. In 1990, the Japanese stock index, the Nikkei 225, plunged by about half. In the period that followed, the excessive property prices also dropped sharply. To date, the Japanese economy has not recovered from the bursting of this bubble. The Nikkei 225 is still far from its highs. At over 200% of GDP, Japan's national debt is significantly higher than that of all other industrialised countries.[10]

Zombie Companies

The debt of Chinese companies amounts to about 19 trillion US dollars, or about 160% of the gross domestic product. In the USA this figure is only around 75%. But while Japanese or US companies generally operate at a profit, an alarmingly high proportion of the Chinese economy consists of Zombie companies that would be insolvent without cheap credit and the will of the government to keep them afloat. But it seems that the willingness to fund those companies is discreasing. In the first two month of 2020 alone, more than 240,000 Chinese companies have filed for bankrupcy.[11] A crisis in China could trigger an unprecedented avalanche. The global economy is much more interconnected today than it was in the early 1990s when the Japanese economy crashed. When the incomparably larger Chinese bubble bursts, the global repercussions are likely to be many times greater.

1.4 A Vicious Circle

The financial crisis, which reached its peak in 2007/2008, began in the USA with the granting of real estate loans to people who could not afford to buy a house. The legal basis for this was the *Housing and Community Development Act* of 1992, which obliged US banks to grant real estate loans to socially disadvantaged people who otherwise would not have the means to buy their own homes. An important role in this played the state-owned credit institutions *Fannie Mae* and *Freddie Mac*, which financed a large part of these properties. These loans were considered secure, as they were covered by real estate, and were packaged in increasingly complicated financial products such as *Credit Default Swaps* or *Collateralised Loan Obligations*. These derivatives were rated AAA by rating agencies like Moody's or Standard & Poors, so they seemed to be a very safe investment.

However, when it became apparent that many of the underlying loans could no longer be serviced, the allegedly risk-free derivatives lost massively in value. As a result, many banks suffered from payment difficulties and stopped lending money to each other. This led to a credit crunch. The global financial system threatened to collapse. In order to prevent this, many banks and insurance companies were rescued with taxpayers' money and partly nationalised, because they were allegedly "systemically relevant" and "too big to fail". One of the few exceptions was the investment bank Lehman Brothers which was allowed to go bankrupt – presumably because many former employees of Lehman's competitor Goldman Sachs were sitting in the US government at the time. So the financial crisis of 2007/2008 was not triggered by alleged "unregulated turbo-capitalism", as some people still believe, but by state intervention in the economy.

Keynes' Obsolete Measures

In order to kick-start the global economy, which slid into recession in 2008, many governments and central banks used the instruments proposed by John Maynard Keynes in the 1930s: Interest rates were cut massively, and the market was flooded with cheap money created out of thin air. In addition, some countries used tax-financed incentives to "stimulate consumption", such as car scrappage schemes in Germany and the USA. The government paid money to anyone who replaced an old car with a new one.

However, word should have gotten around by now that the instruments proposed by Keynes' have no lasting effect, but only cost a lot of money and fizzle out after a short time. They are nevertheless popular with politicians who have no idea about economics. At least they can show their voters that they are doing everything in their power to end the crisis. If only they had more power, how much more could they do!

When Will the Bond Bubble Burst?

To solve the crisis of a monopoly money system caused by state intervention by even more state intervention seems like squaring the circle. Since 2008, central banks have massively bought government and corporate bonds for freshly printed money. Instead of reforming this sick, debt-based sick system at its root, more and more debt was piled up. In 2008, the amount of public and private debt in the USA amounted to 173 trillion US dollars; by 2019 it had already grown to 250 trillion dollars.[12] The measures taken by politicians are like putting out a fire with petrol. "Bond yields worldwide are the lowest in 500 years of history," says star investor Bill Gross. "There are $10 trillion worth of bonds with negative interest rates – this is a supernova that will one day explode."[13]

Since 2008, the central banks have lowered the key interest rates more and more. The interest rates for some government bonds are now even negative. This means that the government even makes money when it borrows something. The commercial banks have to pay penalty fees on their deposits with the central banks instead of receiving interest on them, as would be natural. The first banks have already started to pass this negative interest on to their customers. This means that interest has lost its natural economic function.

The Purpose of Interest

People generally value the earlier fulfilment of a need more highly than a later one. This is precisely what the *Time Preference* expresses, a central concept in the interest theory of the Austrian School of Economics, which was mainly formulated by Eugen Böhm von Bawerk. Time Preference

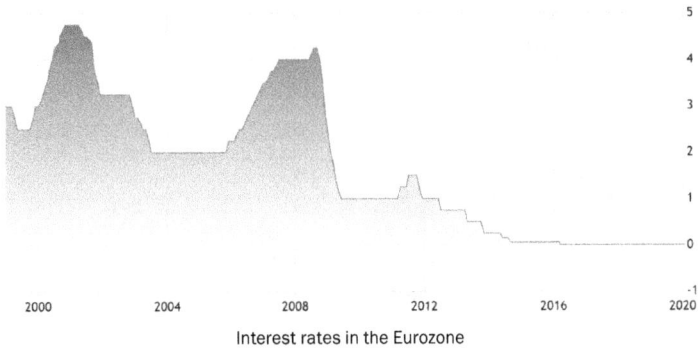

Interest rates in the Eurozone

and natural interest are always positive. 1000 dollars are valued higher today than 1000 dollars in one year. I would only lend it (unless to a very good friend) if I received a higher amount like 1100 dollars when the loan is paid back.

In a market economy system, in which the interest rate can form freely and unhindered within the market, a negative interest rate would be unthinkable. But in the monetary Socialism of our time, the interest rate is not created by supply and demand; it is set by a central government authority, just like the price of a Lada car in the Soviet Union.

The buyers of government bonds with negative yields are usually large pension funds or insurance companies. They are legally obliged to invest a part of their customers' money in "safe" asset classes such as government bonds; otherwise they would probably not do so. Finance ministers benefit from low or negative interest rates: they have to repay less money than they borrowed. But even companies

37

that should have filed for bankruptcy long ago can keep themselves alive by borrowing at low or negative interest rates. Such *Zombie companies* are problematic. The resources that are needed to keep insolvent companies artificially alive could be better used elsewhere.

In many countries, the share of Zombie companies in the economy is now in double figures; in the USA it is estimated at around 10%, in Germany at around 15%, in Greece at over 30%.[14] According to the economist Joseph Schumpeter, a free market economy lives from "creative destruction". Unfortunately, the natural self-healing powers of the market are largely overridden by the monopoly money system and harmful political intervention.[15, 16]

Harming Savers and Tenants

Low and negative interest rates are particularly harmful to savers. Their money loses its value due to inflation, as interest rates on savings accounts are lower than the rate of price increases. Savings are expropriated insidiously when interest rates are low, and even more so when interest rates are negative. Other classic forms of investment such as government bonds are no longer profitable either. Those who are not prepared to invest in riskier assets such as shares or cryptocurrencies have hardly any alternative today. As real estate is still considered a relatively safe investment, a large part of the money pumped into the market is therefore invested in real estate, which drives up prices. As a result, rents are also rising. Politicians who demand a rent cap, as the National Socialists introduced it in Germany in 1936, may be popular with voters, but they are doing even more damage. Who will invest in the construction of new properties if you lose money with it? But if new buildings are not built, the supply remains too low, and prices rise even further. If it is forbidden to ask for higher rents, the houses rot, just as one could observe in Socialist East Germany, which maintained the National Socialists' rent control practice.

Will Cash be banned?

Politicians and central bankers understandably have no interest in raising interest rates because the financial system would then get into unforeseeable difficulties. They prefer to enforce zero and negative interest rates. But who would leave their money in a bank account at negative interest rates? It is more reasonable to withdraw it and store it in cash under the mattress; but if everyone did that, the fractional reserve system would collapse. To prevent this, many politicians are calling for the abolition of cash. In Sweden they have already almost succeeded.

A cash ban will not come overnight, but in small steps so that people get used to it.[17] Fees for withdrawing cash from ATMs will be increased significantly, so that people prefer to pay by bank transfer or cash card rather than in cash. The limits up to which one can legally pay with cash are also falling. In Italy it is forbidden to pay anything in cash for more than 1000 euros. In Germany, the upper limit for the anonymous purchase of gold in cash has been lowered from 10,000 to 2,000 euros. In order to enforce all this, bogus arguments such as the financing of terrorism, drug trafficking or money laundering are being used. Since the Coronavirus panic, the risk of viral infection through bank notes has also been cited as an argument. But the real reason is to prevent an escape from the banking system. Fortunately, for the freedom-loving citizen who does not want his cash banned, there is now an alternative: digital, non-governmental cash. More on this in Chapters 2 and 3.

The Banks' Dilemma

The banks are suffering from the low interest rates as well. Making money out of nothing and then charging interest on it is actually a fantastic business model. But when interest rates are so low that they no longer cover costs, it does not pay off anymore. The loans the commercial banks have granted are yielding less and less profit. As a result, many banks write off losses and use up their equity. However, their equity ratio – i.e. the relation of their equity to their total capital – must not be less than a certain percentage defined by law, otherwise they would have to file for insolvency. Banks must therefore reduce loans rather than grant new ones to prevent their equity ratio from falling below the critical limit.

The central banks' traditional programmes to boost the economy are therefore fizzling out, because the banks cannot convert the central banks' money into loans. The creation of new money out of nothing does not have the desired positive effect anymore. The above-mentioned zombie companies are finding it increasingly difficult to obtain new loans, so they will become insolvent. In addition, following the financial crisis of 2008, politicians have introduced many new regulations, which result in higher costs. Many employees in banks and financial companies are not working productively, but only to comply with legal regulations. These regulations prevent competition because only few start-ups in the financial sector can afford their high costs.

The banks are in a dilemma: if interest rates remain that low, they cannot make money with their core business. But if the central banks raise interest rates, the commercial banks will also have problems. They have granted many loans at a low fixed interest rate that is guaranteed for several years, financed with short-term loans. This is not very reasonable, but common practice. If interest rates rise, banks can slide into the red figures if the interest rate paid by the borrower is lower than their now increased borrowing costs. If interest rates were to return to normal after a period of fixed interest rates, the interest burden on the homebuilder would suddenly increase dramatically. Many borrowers would then probably go broke, which would also not be good news for the banks.

From Bank Crisis to State Bankruptcy

If the zombie companies no longer receive loans, they will have to go into bankruptcy. This would normally be a natural and even healthy process, but when many companies go bankrupt at once, the problems pile up. When loans default, the banks only hold the collateral that the companies have deposited, such as real estate or bonds, which the banks will try to sell in order to get at least some money from the defaulted loan. But if many companies go bankrupt at the same time, many banks will simultaneously try to throw the collaterals onto the market, which logically causes their prices to fall.

In such a negative price spiral, the interbank market also comes to a standstill. The banks will no longer lend each other money. Many banks will go bankrupt and try to be rescued by the government with tax money because they are "systemically relevant", as we experienced during the last financial crisis. But unlike in 2008, many governments are now so heavily indebted that they can no longer issue new bonds. Their tax revenues are not sufficient to service their interest and principal payments. Hardly anyone would buy new bonds from a state threatened with bankruptcy. Also the interest rates on its bonds from the past are rising, so that state bankruptcies are inevitable.

So far, we have only seen state bankruptcies in a few cases, such as Argentina or Lebanon. However, if many states go bankrupt at once, the World Bank and the International Monetary Fund, which normally intervene in such situations, will also run short of funds. In the Eurozone, even countries that are still considered sound, such as Germany, Finland or the Netherlands, will be dragged into insolvency, as they are jointly liable for the debts of the other Euro states. The governments can then only finance themselves by expropriating citizens and companies.

The Corona Panic

The spread of SARS-CoV-2, commonly referred to as "The Coronavirus", has dramatically increased the probability of a major economic crisis. I prefer to leave it to the experts to discuss how dangerous or harmless this virus really is and what should be done to keep it from spreading. Opinions on this vary widely. I also do not want to participate in speculations that the virus panic was artificially staged in order to find a culprit for an inevitable economic crisis. However, without a doubt the measures taken by many governments in response to the threat of the virus, all those curfews, border closures, bans on events and shutdowns of restaurants, cafés and shops, have put the economic existence of many people at risk. Healthy companies went bankrupt because they did not have enough reserves to bridge their losses during the state-imposed lockdown. Who could have foreseen such a thing? Freelancers have lost a large part of their income. Larger companies switched to short-time work or laid off employees.

In order to rescue ailing companies and to support people in need, many governments have set up gigantic stimulus programmes. This is understandable, but in the long term it will have serious consequences for the financial system. The "cure" will probably be much more damaging than the disease itself. As part of its *Pandemic Emergency Purchase Programme (PEPP)*, the European Central Bank buys 750 billion euros worth of government bonds, which means that it creates new money out of nothing and lends it to governments at no cost.[18] The USA are pumping two trillion newly generated US dollars into the economy.[19]

And that is probably just the beginning. The already high national debt of the USA will thus increase massively once again. You should be aware what these measures mean for all holders of euros or US dollars: their income and savings will lose in value, because the inflation of the money supply will cause prices to rise and the purchasing power of money to decline. The USA can afford such a gigantic debt only because the dollar is the world's currency. A large part of international trade is conducted through it. Saudi Arabia and the other OPEC states have their oil paid for exclusively in US dollars. The demand for money that the US Federal Reserve can create out of thin air is therefore guaranteed for the foreseeable future.

All other governments do not have this luxury. Most Eurozone states are already so heavily in debt that large rescue packages are actually beyond their means. Many developing countries are hit even harder because their national debts are often denominated in US dollars. Before they let their people starve, they will probably get into debt anyway. Further state bankruptcies are therefore pre-programmed.

It has hard to predict for which reason the debt-based financial system will collapse. Maybe the Corona panic or the Euro crisis will be the trigger, maybe the China bubble will burst, maybe banks will go bankrupt because their business model is no longer worthwhile. Perhaps it will all happen at the same time. In any case, it would be highly unreasonable not to prepare yourself against a major crash.

2. Digital Cash

As we have seen in Chapter 1, it is not a good idea to trust governments and banks when it comes to money. Especially in the upcoming economic crisis it would be very risky to leave your money in a bank account, where it will lose value every day, or even to invest it into dubious financial products like government bonds with negative interest rates. We need an alternative system that allows us to store and use money without having to rely on banks, credit card companies and government authorities.

Bitcoin was invented precisely for this purpose. In times of crisis, it is an excellent tool to protect us from unwanted restrictions. Bitcoin is immune against confiscations, expropriations and other criminal activities by the powerful.

Of course, cryptocurrencies also have their disadvantages and risks, which we will discuss later. But the advantages they offer for our financial freedom are immense.

At first, we need to understand the basics of this new type of money. I am taking Bitcoin as an example, because it is the "mother of all cryptocurrencies" and by far the most widely used one. There are many hundreds of other cryptocoins that work quite similar to Bitcoin. If you want to know more about them and get to know the different types, you can find this information in my book *Cryptocoins – Investing in Digital Currencies.*

2.1 The Basics of Digital Money

On 3 January 2009, shortly after the financial crisis of 2008, a project was launched that received little attention at the time: Bitcoin. But as we will see, it has the potential to change the world, especially in view of the current crisis. It is based on a whitepaper published by a certain Satoshi Nakamoto on 31 October, 2008, on a mailing list for cryptography experts. He called it *Bitcoin: A Peer-to-Peer Electronic Cash System.*[1]

The term *peer-to-peer* refers to a computer network in which all connected computers are of equal rank ("peers"). Each computer is both sender and receiver. There are no hierarchical differences as with other networks consisting of the computers of normal users (*clients*) and the higher-level *servers*. Peer-to-peer networks have proven to be particularly resistant to attacks and are therefore increasingly popular in the computer world.

"Cash is Printed Freedom"

But what is electronic or digital cash? Most people understand cash as something that they can see and touch, for example in the form of coins or notes. But this is not the main criterion that distinguishes cash from other forms of money. As we have seen in Chapter 1.3, the money in "our" bank account does not belong to us at all. It is merely a claim on the bank, which gives us the more or less credible promise to pay it back.

Cash, on the other hand, is undoubtedly our property. We can use it as we please and are not dependent on the services of third parties. "Cash is printed freedom" is a popular saying, but this is not really true in the case of state monopoly money. A Venezuelan, whose paper money loses value every day, will not believe in such a statement.

With the increasing spread of the Internet in the 1990s, many computer experts have tried to invent digital money that can be sent over the Internet with the same characteristics as cash. It must be clear and comprehensible for everyone whose property it is. And: it must be possible to transfer ownership of it as easily as with a banknote that you hand over to the new owner, despite a distance of several thousand kilometres between sender and recipient.

Bitcoin's Precursors

Early on, Internet pioneers began to use cryptography for the verification and transmission of digital property. They used digital keys to prove ownership of a "digital coin". Digital keys were also used to sign off transfers to other users, i.e. to transfer ownership of their digital coins. One of the first forms of digital cash was Ecash by David Chaum[2], using principles he had already described in a scientific paper in 1983. With his company Digicash, he operated Ecash as a commercial enterprise in the 1990s, albeit without much success.

Other precursor projects to Bitcoin were *HashCash* by Adam Back[3], *B-Money* by Wei Dai[4] and *Bitgold* by Nick Szabo[5]. All of them relied on cryptography. However, they did not get beyond an early stage. We can assume that Satoshi Nakamoto knew these early projects. He explicitly mentioned HashCash and B-Money in his white paper.

David Chaum, Wei Dai, Nick Szabo, Adam Back

The Double Spending Problem

There was one problem that none of Bitcoin's predecessors could solve: the double spending problem. What does this mean? With digital items, the original is as good as the copy. You can make an infinite number of copies of digital files without loss of quality. This is great for music or video files (at least from the user's point of view) but for money it would be disastrous. Money that can be copied an infinite number of times has no value; there would be hyperinflation in no time. So Ecash and other Bitcoin predecessors could not do without a central server where all transfers were registered to ensure the user could only spend a digital coin once. However, Satoshi Nakamoto's goal was to create a fully decentralised system in which no third parties had to be trusted. He wanted to avoid any central institution which is vulnerable to manipulation. His decentralised digital cash system had to function without the need to trust anyone.

The Blockchain

Satoshi's solution was to record all transfers in a kind of "digital ledger", later known as a *Blockchain*. This term, which is so fashionable today, does not appear in the Bitcoin white paper. A Blockchain is a simple database, which is stored decentrally on many thousands of computers. If someone were to try to forge this ledger in his favour, he would have to do so in many thousands of places at the same time. A process called *Proof of Work*, which requires a lot of computing power, ensures that there is only one valid version of the Blockchain at any given time. All parties involved use this procedure to agree on the latest version, even if they do not know or trust each other. Anyone who provides computing power for this purpose is called a *miner.*

Each miner receives the latest transactions from the network, checks whether they are correct and then writes them into a list called a *block*, which also contains a time stamp and refers to the previous block. The blocks are therefore arranged chronologically and form a chain — the Blockchain. The block's data is now used for a complicated cryptographic puzzle.[6] The miner who solves it first may attach his new block to the Blockchain. If one miner claims that he has found the solution, all others check whether this is true. It is difficult to solve the task, but very easy to prove it.

If it is correct, all other miners discard the block they have been working on and move on to the next one, hoping to win the race this time. The miner who has "found the block" is rewarded with the newly mined Bitcoins. This is important, because the miners have relatively high costs for the purchase and operation of their computers. They need a financial incentive to keep the system running.

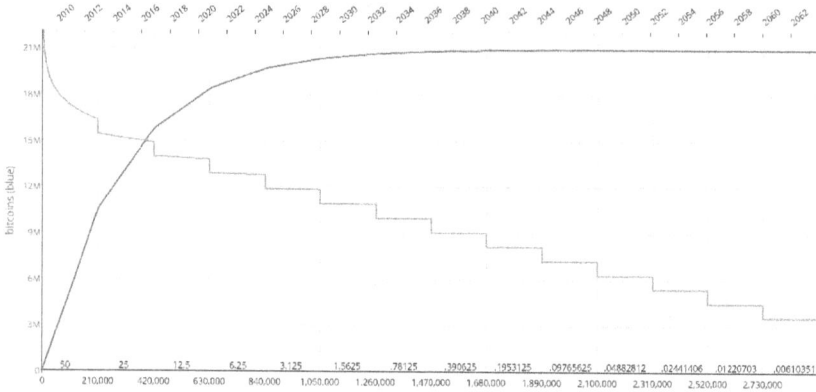

Bitcoin inflates in a predictable way

The Blockchain is Satoshi Nakamoto's major innovation. All other components were known beforehand and already used in previous projects. Satoshi simply combined them in a clever way. But with the invention of the Blockchain, Bitcoin has stepped out of the idea stage, unlike its predecessors, to write an almost unbelievable success story: Bitcoin's price has risen from fractions of cents in the early years, through one dollar at the beginning of 2011, to its all-time-high of almost 20,000 US dollars in December 2017. Even if the price has since fallen, anyone who joined Bitcoin in the early days is likely to be a millionaire today.

The Halving Process

Approximately every ten minutes, the Bitcoin network generates new coins that are distributed to the miners.

They are rewarded for keeping the network alive. In the Bitcoin ecosystem there is no central authority that could punish anyone for fraudulent activities. Satoshi's main focus was to create a system in which even malicious players benefit from playing by the rules. Bitcoin is designed in such a way that it is very difficult, if not impossible, to cheat the system.

In the early days of Bitcoin, the block reward was 50 Bitcoins for each new block. In November 2012 it was halved to 25, and in July 2016 to 12.5 Bitcoins. The most recent halving took place in May 2020. Since then miners receive 6.25 Bitcoins for each block they find.[7] Unlike government money, which can be generated arbitrarily by the central bank, the increase in the Bitcoin money supply is precisely predictable and cannot be changed. In total, there can only be 64 halvings, so the maximum amount of Bitcoins is just a bit under 21 million. This will probably be reached by 2140. As of June 2020, more than 18.5 million Bitcoins have already been mined. Satoshi Nakamoto has designed Bitcoin to be extremely scarce, even scarcer than gold (more on this in Chapter 3).

It is quite possible that Satoshi knew the works of Ludwig von Mises and modelled his invention after gold. This is by no means self-evident. Many economists, such as the monetarists around Milton Friedman, believe that the money supply should grow with the economy. In today's mainstream economics, the prevailing doctrine is to let the money supply grow by 2% every year, regardless of the size of the economy, because "a little inflation boosts consumption". The economists of the Austrian School, to which Mises, Hayek and Böhm-Bawerk belong (see Chapter 4), consider this to be nonsense. For them, precious metals, which are scarce by nature, serve best as money – they did not yet know of the even scarcer Bitcoin.

Private and Public Keys

We have already heard that cryptocurrencies use cryptography to prove ownership, hence their name. They use the principle of *asymmetric encryption*, which you may know from scrambling emails. For this you do not use just a single encryption key, but a pair of keys. It consists of a private key and the corresponding public key. You can send the public key via an open medium like the Internet. If it falls into the hands of criminals, it does not matter. It can only be used to send an encrypted e-mail to the owner of the key. If the recipient wants to read the email, he needs the corresponding private key. If you don't have it, you will only see a jumble of letters and numbers.

It's similar with Bitcoin: You need the public key, or more precisely the Bitcoin address generated from it,[8] to send money to someone. The recipient needs the matching private key to access the money and to sign a new transaction. You should therefore keep your private key top secret and never give it to anyone else. Whoever has your private key has the power to spend your money. Or, to use a typical Bitcoin saying: *NOT YOUR KEYS, NOT YOUR COINS!* I deliberately write in plural because you can own an infinite number of these key pairs. I recommend that you use a new Bitcoin address for each transaction. This has to do with protecting your privacy, which we will discuss in more detail in Chapter 3.

The Bitcoin Wallet

As a normal user you hardly ever see your private keys. All keys, whether private or public, are managed by a piece of software called a *wallet*. The term "key ring" would actually be more appropriate, because the Bitcoins themselves are not stored in the wallet, as the term suggests. They live on the Blockchain, which is distributed to thousands of computers on the Internet. What the wallet contains are your public and private keys.

So called *full node wallets* download the complete Blockchain, which may take some time due to the large amount of data. Therefore most of today's wallets are *light wallets*. They connect and synchronise with a full node on the Internet, which is sufficient for most applications. By using a Light Wallet, you do not have to download the Blockchain first, but can start immediately.

2.2 How to Use Bitcoin?

The first thing you need to use Bitcoin is your own wallet. Wallets are available for all common operating systems, whether Windows, Mac or Linux for the computer, or Android and IoS for the mobile phone. You simply download them from the provider's website, or for your mobile phone, from the Google PlayStore or the Apple AppStore.[9]

The wallet is free of charge. You don't have to fill out an application form, as with a bank account, and you don't need anyone's permission to use it. Every Internet user can become a Bitcoin user within minutes. This is especially important for the billions of people in the world who do not have a bank account and would not easily get one. Smartphones with Internet access, on the other hand, are now widely used also in developing countries, so billions of people can now use Bitcoin, which literally knows no borders. There are multi-wallets that allow you to use not only Bitcoin, but also other crypto currencies. Each of the countless cryptocoins also have their own wallets.

Sending Bitcoins

All wallets differ only slightly in their use. The most important functions are *sending* and *receiving* money. To send Bitcoins to someone, click on the tab or button *SEND* and enter the recipient's address in the address field. The

SEND function of a typical Bitcoin Wallet

address is a sequence of numbers, upper- and lower-case letters, which might look like this:

3x5tJVnGLC2Uiqg3c7U6i2EaPezq4q3Rjd

You will probably not type it in, but rather copy and paste it, for example from the recipient's website or from an email. You can also scan a QR code that contains the same information, which is especially handy when using a mobile phone. In another field you enter the amount you want to send. When scanning a QR code, the recipient can already specify the amount, so this step is not necessary.

Finally, you select how much you want to pay for as a fee for the transfer. This fee is paid to the miner who finds the corresponding block. If you are not in a hurry, you can select a low fee. The higher the fee, the faster the transaction is confirmed by the Bitcoin network, because the miners naturally prefer to include high fee transfers into their blocks. Then you click *OK* or *SEND* and shortly afterwards the recipient will see in his wallet that the money is on its way to him. Once the transaction has been sent from your wallet to the Bitcoin network, it is irrevocably stored in one of the next blocks.

Receiving Bitcoins

If you want to receive money, you click on the tab or button *RECEIVE*. Then a Bitcoin address and the corresponding QR code will be displayed. You copy this address and send it to the person from whom you expect a payment. If the sender is directly in front of you, show him the QR code so that he can scan it with his mobile phone. It is best to have a new address generated every time. There are virtually infinite numbers of them. As mentioned before, I recommend to use a new Bitcoin address for every transaction to protect your privacy.

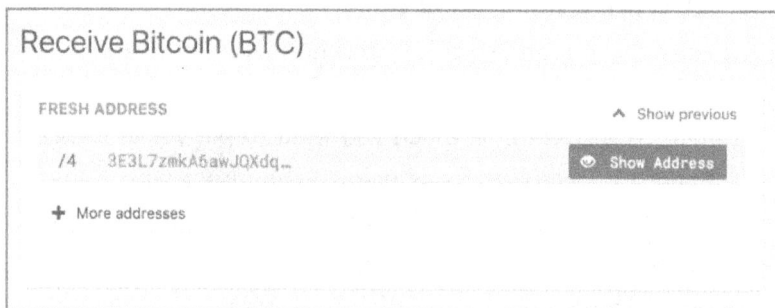

Receive Bitcoin (BTC)

FRESH ADDRESS   ∧ Show previous

/4   3E3L7zmkA6awJQXdq...   ⊙ Show Address

+ More addresses

RECEIVE function of a typical Bitcoin Wallet

When the sender has sent his transfer, it will be displayed in your wallet immediately afterwards and confirmed after some time (see *SEND*). If this does not happen, but the sender claims to have paid, there is a simple method to check it: You enter the address in a so-called Block Explorer like Blockchain.info or Blockchair.com. There you can see whether the money has actually been sent and confirmed. The names of the senders and recipients are of course not displayed, but if you know a concrete Bitcoin address, you can see which inputs and outputs are listed on it. Blind trust is not necessary with Bitcoin. Everything can be verified.

Using Bitcoin is very easy with today's wallets. No special computer knowledge is required. The only thing you need to get used to are the long Bitcoin addresses. But honestly, the IBAN numbers that have replaced the account numbers are not that much easier either. They are much too complicated to remember. I suppose you don't know your IBAN number by heart, like your account number in the old days. You will probably copy and paste it just like a Bitcoin address. Whether the address is a bit longer and more complicated doesn't really matter for the usage. The advantage of Bitcoin addresses is: they are very secure. Guessing a Bitcoin address by chance is mathematically extremely unlikely. It is virtually impossible, as it would take many human lifetimes.

Programmable Money

An important difference to conventional money: Bitcoin is programmable. Each transaction can contain programme code that defines it more precisely. For example, you can specify that a transaction be made at a specific time. Or: it must be signed not only with one, but with several digital keys. This is called a *Multi-Signature*, or *Multi-Sig*. Of course you do not have to program this yourself. With a multi-sig-wallet you can define it conveniently via its user interface. For example, you can specify that two out of three key holders must sign the transaction to be valid (or three out of three, four out of five, seven out of ten ... any combination is possible). This can be very useful, for example, if you have a company with several directors or if you share a wallet with your spouse.

Multi-Sig is also useful for security. If a thief steals one of your keys, he still cannot access your money. He would have to get a hold of one or more other keys. Companies that offer secure storage of Bitcoins as a service usually use the multi-sig feature.

Multi-signatures are also used for conflict resolution in e-commerce. Buyer and seller agree on a 2-out-of 3 Multi-Sig with a neutral arbitrator holding the third key. If the buyer and seller agree that everything is correct, the arbitrator does not need to do anything, because two keys are sufficient to release the money already paid by the buyer. But in case of disagreement, the arbitrator can use his third key to reach a decision. He can, for example, take the side of the buyer who claims never to have received the goods, or that of the seller if he can prove that he delivered them correctly. For this service the arbitrator receives a predetermined fee.

In a decentralised cash system, neutral arbitration service can be very important, because there is no bank or credit card company to call in case of conflict. These companies charge high, often hidden, fees for their arbitration. In the Bitcoin space there is a free market for neutral arbitrators whose fees are transparent. You can choose to forgo their services and save money, or to use them voluntarily and pay for them.

The Lightning Network

In many cases, transfers that take a few minutes or hours and cost a few cents may be perfectly fine. If you are sending large amounts of money from continent to continent, it is much faster and cheaper than in the old banking system. But for certain cases this is not enough, especially for buying everyday goods for smaller amounts. If you want to quickly pay for a coffee in the café around the corner, you certainly won't want to wait ten minutes for the transaction to be confirmed by the network, because then the coffee will be cold. And with a value of two to three dol-

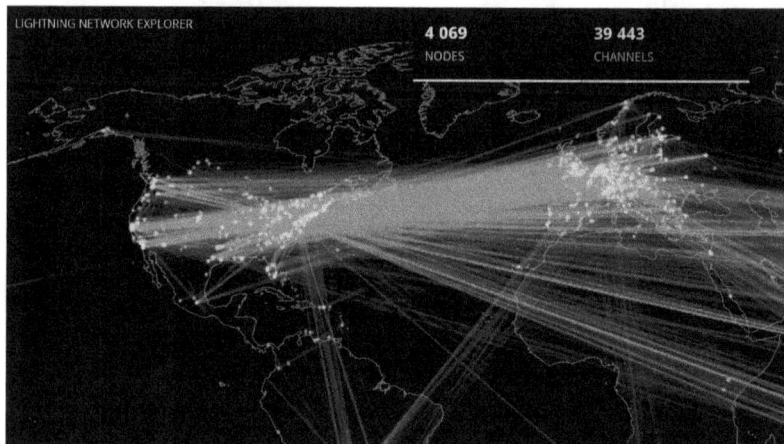

Nodes of the Lightning Network

lars, even a fee of a few cents per transaction would be far too expensive.

To solve this problem, a new invention called the *Lightning Network* is currently being developed. It forms a second layer above the Bitcoin Network, and is characterised by transactions which only take fractions of a second (they are "as fast as lightning"), at a cost of only a fraction of a cent. This is achieved by not storing every single transaction in the Blockchain, which is relatively slow and costly due to its characteristics described in 2.1. Instead, many transactions are processed off-chain, i.e. outside the Blockchain, via so-called *Payment Channels*. These were originally designed so that two users can send payments to each other, only the result is registered in the Blockchain. The Lightning Network combines many of these channels into a network through which it is potentially possible to reach many people. It works similarly to e-mail, which also finds its way via the Internet through many nodes until the final recipient. As complex as this process is, the e-mail user does not need to care about it. He writes his mail and clicks *SEND*, the rest is being handled in the background.

That's how elegantly the Lightning Network is supposed to function one day. It is not yet ready for market, but many software developers are working on eliminating the weaknesses it undoubtedly still has, and it is progressing quickly and promisingly. Many Bitcoiners see the Lightning Network as the "new big thing" which will help Bitcoin achieve its breakthrough – much like the World Wide Web did for the Internet. The Web's colourful graphics and ease of use has made the underlying Internet and its TCP/IP protocol, which before could only be used by computer nerds, accessible to a mass audience. Another advantage of Lightning is that – unlike the classic Bitcoin network – transactions are completely anonymous.

2.3 How to Fill Your Bitcoin Wallet

The best way to get Bitcoins is to earn them through your own work. If you want to prepare for a collapse of the current financial system (and why else would you read this book?), you should get used to accepting Bitcoin right now. You can assume that after the crash – apart from primitive bartering – there will hardly be any other way to trade with other people. In this respect, it is helpful if you start using Bitcoins now, not only after the collapse. When it comes to security (more on this in Section 2.4), there is still a lot to learn. It is better to be able to do this now in a relaxed manner.

It is very likely that the purchasing power of each Bitcoin will increase due to its scarcity. Every Bitcoin you earn now will probably be worth significantly more in the future. If you accept Bitcoin, you are actively contributing to its increase in value. Money ultimately only gets its value from being used as such. Even gold would be worth nothing if people refused to accept it as payment for their work.

As an Entrepreneur or Freelancer

If you are a freelancer or self-employed, you should definitely offer Bitcoin as a payment option to your clients. You only need to provide them with a Bitcoin address. If your client is not yet willing or able to use Bitcoin directly, you can use the Swiss provider *Intarium.ch*. They accept your customer's fiat money and pay you (for a fee of 1.97%) directly in good, hard Bitcoins.

If you run your own shop, whether in the real world or online, I also recommend that you accept Bitcoin. There are specialised companies that offer Bitcoin integration conveniently, such as *Bitpay*, *Bitgo* or *Coinbase*. By using their software, an invoice and a new Bitcoin address are automatically generated for each purchase. These service providers also offer to immediately exchange your Bitcoins into dollars or euros and transfer them to your bank account. Of course, you should not use this option, or only to the extent that you absolutely need fiat money. You usually have the option to have part of your money paid out in fiat and part in Bitcoins. The higher the Bitcoin part, the better.

But you do not really need fiat money that often. For example, if you receive an invoice and the biller refuses to accept Bitcoin, you can have the Swiss service provider *Lamium* settle the invoice in Euros and pay for it in Bitcoin. There are many providers of credit or debit cards that you can top up with Bitcoin and pay via the old system while it still works. And if you really need some government cash, you can easily exchange small amounts privately at a Bitcoin meetup (see: *Buying Bitcoins*). You should already get used to using the soon to be obsolete banking system as little as possible.

As an Employee

If you are employed, it may be a little more difficult to persuade your employer to pay you in Bitcoins. However, if you choose to have as much financial freedom as possible, being an employee, with its many restrictions, is not the best option anyway. But here too, a service provider can help. If you register with *Bitwage.com*, your employer can transfer your salary through the old banking system, and you will receive it from Bitwage in Bitcoin. The employer does not need to register with Bitwage, or pay in Bitcoin, he is simply given the bank details and pays in fiat. The fees depend on the type of payment method you choose.

Buying Bitcoins

There are numerous exchanges where you can get rid of your fiat money and exchange it for Bitcoins. Some of the best known are *Kraken, Bitstamp* and *Binance*. The problem with all these services: they are required to check and store your personal data and to disclose them to the authorities if they ask for it. You have to upload a picture of your ID card, often a selfie on which you hold your ID card in your hand. Your privacy is therefore not protected here.

You can avoid this if you use a decentralised exchange such as *Bisq*, which is a bit more complicated to use, but does-not require those anti-privacy actions. In many countries around the world there are Bitcoin ATMs where you can buy Bitcoins up to a certain amount without presenting documents.

Through *LocalBitcoins.com* you can find people almost any-where in the world with which you can privately exchange

Bitcoins for monopoly money. The advantage of this is that you can purchase Bitcoins legally without any governmental authority finding out about it. However, there is the risk that the buyer will cheat you and run away with the cash.

To mitigate that risk, use the Meetup.com platform or a general Internet search to find out if there is a Bitcoin meetup in your city. Most major cities now have such meetings where Bitcoin fans can exchange ideas and get to know each other. Most likely you will find someone there who will sell you Bitcoins for cash, especially if it is not a large amount. A Bitcoin meetup offers a certain degree of protection, as members usually know each other and can recommend trustworthy sellers. And if someone really runs away with your cash, it's easier to stop him at such a meetup than in a place where people don't know each other.

2.4 Storing Bitcoins Securely

Bitcoin is cash, which means: you are 100% responsible for it yourself – just as you are responsible for the banknotes you carry in your wallet. There is no bank you can call to cancel a transfer, no credit card company that would block a stolen card and replace payments already made. A Bitcoin payment is irrevocable. You should not behave the way you do in the old world of banking. Do not leave your

Bitcoins on an account at a Bitcoin exchange. It might happen that they are gone if the exchange is hacked. In the early days of Bitcoin, this unfortunately happened many times. The most spectacular case was the hack of the long dominant Bitcoin exchange Mt.Gox in February 2014, when 850,000 Bitcoins were allegedly stolen. At today's rate (June 2020) that would be over 7.8 billion US dollars.

Never Entrust Your Keys to Anyone!

Today's exchanges have much better security measures than Mt.Gox, which was originally designed as a trading platform for fantasy playing cards.[10] When Mt.Gox was relaunched as a Bitcoin exchange in 2010, a Bitcoin was only worth fractions of cents. Given this low value, security concerns were hardly an issue. Today, exchange operators invest significantly more in security measures. Nevertheless, absolute IT security cannot exist; Bitcoin exchanges can and will be hacked.

Of course, banks are also often targets of malicious hacker attacks; they just keep this secret to avoid any panic. But the bank does not really keep "your money" in "your account", it simply keeps a record of how much it owes you. If a hacker penetrates a bank's system, the original condition of your account can be restored without any problems. A Bitcoin exchange cannot do this. If a hacker steals Bitcoins, it's like he enters the bank's vault and steals gold bars. If you use an exchange to exchange your fiat money for Bitcoin, you should transfer the Bitcoins from there to your own wallet immediately.

Remember: Only if you control your private keys yourself you really own the Bitcoins. Never, really: NEVER store your Bitcoins (or strictly speaking: your private keys) for a long time on other people's servers, only on your own devices. Still, your own computer can also be hacked, although it may not be as worthwhile a target for hackers as an exchange, which manages millions or even billions of dollars of Bitcoins. But any device connected to the Internet can be hacked. There are two ways to prevent this.

Paper Wallets

A relatively secure, though cumbersome form of Bitcoin storage is a so-called paper wallet. It is a piece of paper with the private key and corresponding Bitcoin address printed on it, together with their QR codes. You can scan the QR code of the Bitcoin address and transfer Bitcoins to it. To get the money back, you need the private key, which you scan from the paper wallet and enter into an electronic wallet. However, this is only possible with the entire amount, so paper wallets are not practical for daily use. Paper wallets have other disadvantages, which is why I do not recommend this method, especially to beginners. For example, if you have your keys generated by a paper wallet provider on the Internet, they can be stolen. The internal memory of the printer could also contain your private key and be read by hackers. There are ways to avoid this, but it would take some effort. For example, you would not be allowed to use the normal operating system of your computer (it might already be hacked), but would have to start a new one via CD / DVD.

An alternative is the *Entropy* device offered by the wallet provider Mycelium, which you connect directly to the USB port of your printer. The keys are generated in the Entropy and printed out directly, so hackers cannot get them. But if you were willing to buy a special device to secure your Bitcoins, I would rather recommend a hardware wallet.

Hardware Wallets

Hardware wallets are small gadgets on which you can store your private keys. They are also used to sign transactions. A hardware wallet plugs into your computer's USB port and works in combination with its own web wallet or other software wallets. If you want to transfer Bitcoins, you need to confirm this with your hardware wallet in addition to the procedure described in 2.2. To do this you either press a button or you perform a function on its screen. It then sends the signed transaction to the software wallet, which broadcasts it to the Bitcoin network.

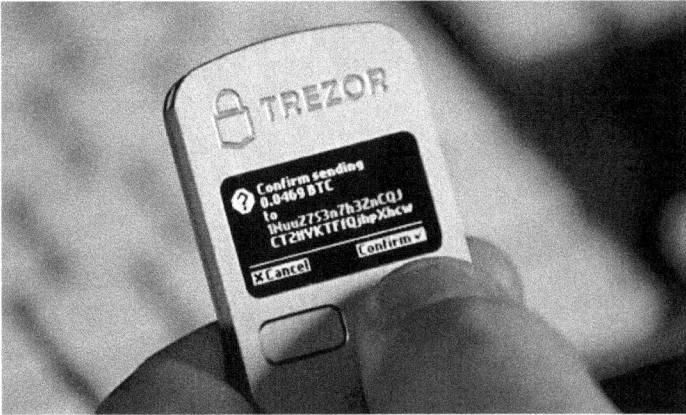

A Hardware Wallet

The private keys never get into your computer, but remain in a protected area on the hardware wallet. Even if your computer is infected by a virus and controlled by malicious hackers, your private keys stay safe. Of course, you have to trust the manufacturer to actually build the devices as secure as they claim. There have been cases of hacked hardware wallets, but the hacker needs access to your device. However, hardware wallets are currently the best way to store Bitcoins and use them in everyday life.

The best-known manufacturers of hardware wallets are *Trezor, Ledger* and *KeepKey*. A relatively new provider is *Digital BitBox*, which advertises with even better security. BitBox comes from Switzerland, which has a good reputation in terms of security and reliability. Its founder Jonas Schnelli is also one of the developers responsible for the further development of the Bitcoin protocol, so you can assume that he knows what he is doing. The various models do not differ significantly in functionality. Hardware wallets are not cheap, the simpler models cost around 50 euros, better-equipped ones, e.g. with a colour touch screen, can cost up to 150 euros. If you only want to exchange a few euros for Bitcoins to try out digital cash, it's not worth the expense. But as soon as you start earning Bitcoins yourself and want to save larger sums, it is very reasonable to invest in security and buy a hardware wallet.

The Seed Phrase

All modern wallets are so-called *Hierarchical Deterministic Wallets* or, in short, HD wallets. This means that all keys generated by it are based on a single cryptographic seed key. You only need to know this seed key, and then all private and public keys can be derived from it. The cryptographic procedure for this is complicated, but it makes securing a wallet much easier. When you set up the wallet for the first time, you write down a so-called seed phrase consisting of 12, 16 or 24 English words. The term "phrase" is a bit misleading, because it is simply a random string of words. Their order is important, but they don't make much sense. A seed phrase could look like this:

watch collapse practice feed shame open despair creek road again ice least

The original seed key can be derived from these words. Don't ask me how to do that. I'm not a cryptographer and fortunately no one has to be one to handle Bitcoin. All you need to do is to write down these words on a piece of paper and hide them in a safe place. Write them down by hand, or with Grandpa's typewriter. Never use a computer or a mobile phone, as both could be hacked. You should guard your seed phrase like Scrooge McDuck guards his money vault. It is the backup copy of your money. No one other than you or people you absolutely trust should get their hands on it. It is advisable to hide several copies in several places so that at least one copy is left in case of a flooding or fire. Some people even use a hammer and letter stencils to engrave their seed phrase in titanium, to make sure it survives water and fire damage.

Analogue is Safer

It almost sounds absurd that digital cash should be stored in such an analogue form, but that is indeed the safest way. If your computer crashes, your mobile phone gets stolen or your dog eats your hardware wallet – stay calm, your Bitcoins are not lost. You can download a new software wallet or buy a new hardware wallet, then select the *Restore Wallet* option. If you now enter the words of your seed phrase in the correct order, the lost coins will magically reappear in your wallet. In fact, the Bitcoins were never gone. Unlike coins and notes, Bitcoins cannot be lost because they are not stored in your wallet, but in the Blockchain. Only the holder of the private keys can access the coins, so you better take care of the keys. You need to make a backup copy of them to get back to your coins. HD wallets, seed keys and seed phrases are probably some of the most useful inventions in the Bitcoin world. Although Bitcoins behave like cash in many ways, they can be backed up. Try this with Euro or Dollar notes!

Now that you've learned how digital cash works and how to best handle it, we want to look at the most important question for this book: how can Bitcoin help you to keep your money safe in a financial crisis?

3. Is Bitcoin Crisis-Proof?

Cryptocurrencies like Bitcoin are still suspicious to many people. Using them as an antidote in case of a financial crisis may seem like a crazy idea. Bitcoin has a rather bad image, it is considered insecure and highly risky. The media usually report on Bitcoin only when an exchange has been hacked or the price slumps dramatically.

This does not sound at all like a "safe haven" in a financial crisis. However, as all too often, media coverage and reality have little to do with each other. It pays to use competent specialist media and not trust unreliable sources like television, newspapers and other mainstream media.

3.1 Why Does Bitcoin Have Value?

Let us first ask ourselves why Bitcoin has any value at all. It has been created just a few years ago, probably by a group of computer nerds. In the first years of its history, Bitcoin was actually worthless. Early adopters sent thousands of Bitcoins back and forth for fun, just to try out if the system worked. Hardly anyone was aware that these would one day be worth millions. Many gave Bitcoins as gifts to friends and acquaintances, simply to advertise them. There were even websites called *Bitcoin Faucets*, where you only had to register to receive Bitcoins for free. Gradually, the first entrepreneurs began to accept Bitcoins for digital products such as virtual private networks or domain addresses. Most of them did so probably for idealistic reasons, not with the aim of making money.

The legendary first purchase of a real good for Bitcoin was probably also more a gag than a serious economic transaction. In May 2010, programmer Laszlo Hanyecz from Florida offered 10,000 Bitcoins to anyone who would deliver two pizzas to him, whether self-baked or ordered. He probably mined these Bitcoins himself on his own computer. At that time, a normal PC was completely sufficient for this. Jeremy 'Jercos' Sturdivant accepted the deal and bought two pizzas for Laszlo from Papa John's with his credit card. The whole process is documented in the forum *Bitcointalk.org*. Laszlo writes there: "I think it would be interesting if I could say that I paid for a pizza in Bit-

The Original Pizzas bought for Bitcoin in May 2010

coins".[1] Today May 22nd is celebrated as *Bitcoin Pizza Day* by Bitcoin fans all over the world by eating pizza. The 10,000 Bitcoins are worth around 95 million US dollars today (June 2020). Quite a sum, but Laszlo Hanyecz has written Bitcoin history with his purchase.

In 2010, *BitcoinMarket* and *Mt. Gox* were the first exchanges where you could buy Bitcoins with US dollars. Both no longer exist. The interest in Bitcoin gradually grew, and with it the price. In the course of 2010 it rose from a few fractions of a US cent to half a dollar. In February 2011, it reached dollar parity for the first time, i.e. one Bitcoin was worth a whole dollar.

When in June 2011 US Senator Chuck Schumer warned on television that Bitcoins could be used to buy drugs anonymously on the Internet, the price skyrocketed to over 30 dollars – the biggest leap Bitcoin has ever made. Since then, the price of Bitcoin jumped up and down like a rollercoaster, but it never dropped below $2 (in December 2011). It reached its all-time high so far at $19,891 in December 2017.

After this brief digression into Bitcoin history, let's get back to the original question: why do Bitcoins have value? The answer to this question is simple. If people are willing to spend money on an item, then it obviously has value. There is no such thing as an "intrinsic", or inner value of a good. Value is something totally subjective. It only arises when people attribute value to something, that is, when they perceive it as useful or enriching for their lives. If that is the case, they are willing to give something else in return, such as money, a barter commodity or work. Over the years, more and more people have chosen to spend money or work on what was originally a worthless digital product. But why? Isn't this all just a speculative bubble? The whim of a few naive computer freaks? A fraudulent pyramid game?

Again, the answer is simple. Things are valuable when they are useful to people. And the scarcer they are, the more valuable they are. Bitcoin is not just a digital currency, but first and foremost a global payment system that has been working reliably for over eleven years now. It offers great advantages over the conventional banking system: Bitcoin enables unconfiscatable, pseudonymous payments to any country in the world, at high speed and at moderate cost. This even includes countries with capital controls or under economic embargo. As this payment service can only be used with the system currency also called Bitcoin, people are willing to spend money on the latter. And since Bitcoin is deliberately kept scarce by design (see 2.1), its value increases the more people use it. This is economic theory for beginners: if the demand for a scarce item grows significantly faster than its supply, its price must rise. Of course, Bitcoin is also an object of speculation: investors speculate that it will become more widespread in the future and thus even more valuable. But Bitcoin has as little in common with a "bubble" or a "pyramid scheme" as the gold standard has with the euro.

3.2 The World's Hardest Money

Satoshi Nakamoto has designed Bitcoin to be even scarcer than gold. New gold mines may be discovered. In the 16th century, the discovery of South America's gold mines led to an oversupply and thus to a fall in gold prices.[2] Theoretically, even a meteorite of pure gold could strike the earth and lead to a new glut of gold – extremely unlikely, but not entirely impossible. Such unforeseeable events, however, can be ruled out with Bitcoin. Due to the halving mechanism described in 2.1, Bitcoin is increasingly approaching its absolute upper limit of 21 million, which will probably

Bitcoin is scarcer than gold

be reached by 2140. There is no realistic way to change this and increase the amount of Bitcoins. Theoretically, it would be possible if a majority of miners were to agree on it. But this will never happen, because no Bitcoin owner has an interest in diluting the value of his coins.

The value of precious metals such as gold, silver or platinum is closely linked to their *stock-to-flow ratio*, i.e. the ratio of their total amount already mined (*stock*) to the units newly mined every year (*flow*). The higher the stock-to-flow ratio of a commodity, the more valuable it is. Until now, gold has been considered the commodity with the highest stock-to-flow ratio. The quantity mined to date is around 178,000 tonnes, with around 2700 tonnes of new gold being added each year. Gold's stock-to-flow ratio is therefore around 66, which theoretically means that it would take 66 years to mine gold to reach the existing quantity.[3] If the aforementioned golden meteorite does not strike the earth, it is more likely that the annual quantity mined will decrease over time, so that the stock-to-flow ratio will continue to increase.

If we apply this model to Bitcoin, we see that Bitcoin will be even scarcer than gold.[4] Since the latest halving, which happened in May 2020, 6.25 new Bitcoins are being mined every ten minutes, i.e. 37.5 per hour, 900 per day, 328,500 per year. Today the amount of existing Bitcoins is about 18.5 million,[5] so its stock-to-flow ratio is 56, almost that of gold. After the next halving, which is expected to take place at the end of 2023, only 164,250 new Bitcoins will be added each year. Bitcoin's stock-to-flow ratio will then be around 116, clearly outperforming gold. By the time of the last halving in 2140, Bitcoin's stock-to-flow ratio will be many times higher than that of gold. So far, the stock-to-flow model has explained Bitcoin's rise surprisingly well. If we extrapolate the previous curve, the Bitcoin price can

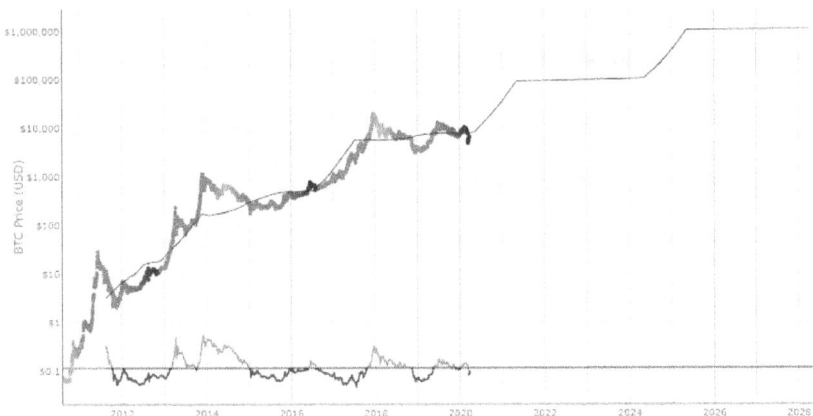

Bitcoin's stock-to-flow ratio

still go up quite a bit. According to this model, in 2022 we would see a price of 100,000 US dollars. In the future it could even reach a million of today's dollars. But maybe the price will then be a trillion dollars, due to the inevitable inflation of fiat money.

We should get used to indicating the price of Bitcoin in gold, which would express its value much better. While fiat currencies lose value over time, experience shows that gold retains its purchasing power. About a hundred years ago, you had to pay about the price of an ounce of gold for a tailor-made men's suit. This still applies today. Although the prices of gold and men's suits, expressed in dollars, are significantly higher, their ratio has remained almost the same. If the value of Bitcoin continues to develop according to its rising stock-to-flow ratio, its value expressed in gold and therefore its purchasing power should increase significantly.

3.3 Bitcoin Cannot be Stopped

Another factor that makes Bitcoin interesting in times of crisis: it is independent of the legacy financial system. If it collapses, Bitcoin will not be affected, at least not negatively. It is even more likely that the Bitcoin price will rise sharply because many people want to put their money in a safe place and choose Bitcoin as an alternative. So it is better to invest in Bitcoin now rather than later, when everyone invests in it and prices will skyrocket. It is very likely that in times of crisis, governments will resort to all kinds of repressive methods to "save the financial system". For example, they will partially expropriate bank customers' assets, as they did in Cyprus in 2013. Or they will freeze accounts and allow holders to withdraw cash only to a limited extent, as they did in Argentina and Greece. Transfers abroad will probably be very strictly controlled and restricted, so that no one can take their money out of the country. This drastic restriction of our freedom is haphazardly called "capital controls".

Bitcoin is immune to all these coercive measures. It is impossible to stop a Bitcoin transfer or to freeze a Bitcoin account. With Bitcoin, you can easily transfer money abroad, even if there are strict capital controls. The government has no chance of finding out how many Bitcoins you own and expropriate them unless it threatens you with force. But it cannot do that to many people. If a lot of people switch to Bitcoin, the government is powerless.

If you decide to move to another country (more on this in Chapter 5), you can easily pass through border controls even with large amounts of Bitcoins. As we learned in Section 2.4, Bitcoins can be saved using just a few English words. All you need to do is hide the paper that contains your seed phrase well. And better do not write "My Bitcoins" above it. You might disguise the random words as a Dadaist poem, or mark them with a pencil in a book as if you were taking notes. In any case, it is much easier to cross borders with Bitcoins than with cash, which can be sniffed out by dogs, or with gold, which can be traced with metal detectors.

Does that sound paranoid to you? You think you'll never need this in your life? I recommend to be prepared for leaving your home with all your belongings and to settle somewhere else. Bitcoin makes this possible in a relatively simple manner. If it does not become necessary after all because the crisis doesn't get too bad or you use other methods to deal with it, all the better, but you should avoid to be surprised by the crisis and lose your savings.

3.4 Bitcoin Works Without Banks

If the current banking system is no longer available, it is important to have a functioning alternative. Bitcoin enables you to trade, buy and sell products, offer your services, pay people for their work, and much more, anywhere in the world. Banks or other middlemen are no longer needed. So even if all banks go bankrupt, we do not have to go back to bartering with all its shortcomings.

Some people feel uncomfortable that Bitcoin needs the Internet and electricity to function. They are afraid that both would be unavailable in a crisis and their money would be gone. I think that risk is very small. The Internet and electricity have become an integral part of our civilization. Without them, many things beyond the Bitcoin network, from power stations to transportation, would not function. Even in difficult times, people will therefore give high priority to a functioning Internet and a reliable electricity supply. Bitcoin could even cope with a temporary blackout. As long as there is only one computer on which the Blockchain is stored, no Bitcoins will be lost. You cannot make normal transfers during a blackout, but you could continue seamlessly as soon as the Internet is up and running again.

It is also possible that Bitcoin works without the normal Internet in the case of a crisis, but uses so-called local mesh networks whose nodes connect directly to each other, for example by radio waves.[6] The company *Blockstream* has built up a network of satellites on which the Bitcoin Blockchain is stored.[7] Local mesh networks can connect to these satellites and thus keep the Bitcoin network alive even if the classic Internet fails.

In principle, it cannot be ruled out that the Bitcoin network will be hacked. Hackers have tried this time and time again. In the eleven years of its existence, however, no hacker attack on Bitcoin has ever been successful. I am not talking about hacks of individual exchanges or other enterprises, but about the Bitcoin network itself. The Bitcoin developers are probably among the most brilliant programmers on the planet. Their working principles are extremely conservative and geared towards the highest possible security. After all, the Bitcoin network now holds amounts worth over 173 billion US dollars. Every innovation is therefore discussed back and forth for a long time and tested many times before it is introduced.

When the crisis breaks out, Bitcoin will most likely experience an enormous influx of new users. Let's hope that this will take some more time and that the Bitcoin network will then be ready and able to withstand this growth spurt. There all still some teething troubles of the new money that need to be dealt with.

3.5 Weaknesses of Bitcoin

With its eleven years, Bitcoin is still a very young phenomenon. By comparison, very few people used the Internet eleven years after its launch in 1969 (then still know as the Arpanet). In 1980, it was hardly known, except by some scientists at universities and research laboratories. You needed computer skills to access it, as the graphical user interface of the World Wide Web was invented only in 1989. It was not until the mid-1990s, at the age of about 25, that the Internet developed into the medium without which we can hardly imagine our lives today.

Bitcoin is Not Widespread Yet

Bitcoin is a bit more widespread, but not very much. It is estimated that about 25 million people worldwide currently use it,[8] which is still very few compared to the more than 7.5 billion people on earth. You can already buy many things with Bitcoin, both online and in the real world, but it is still a long way from being accepted as general payment. This is partly due to the natural inertia of people, who always need some time to get used to new things. On the other hand, Bitcoin still has some weaknesses that need to be overcome for it to really catch on.

Bitcoin is Too Slow

Compared to banking wire transfers, Bitcoin's waiting times are competitive, but for everyday use a Bitcoin transaction takes too long, due to the mining process described in 2.1. No one would wait several hours for a payment to be confirmed in the Blockchain for a purchase. Any seller who does not blindly trust his customers and wants to release the goods without confirmation from the network is dependent on payment providers such as Bitpay who take the risk. But the whole idea of Bitcoin is to work without such middlemen without having to trust anyone. This is where the *Lightning Network* (see Section 2.2), should help. With Lightning, Bitcoin payments are possible in fractions of a second without the need for payment providers.

Bitcoin's Fees Are Too High

Fees are also significantly lower in Lightning than for on-chain Bitcoin payments. This is important, because if the fees are too high, Bitcoin becomes unusable. During the Bitcoin boom at the end of 2017, when many new users discovered Bitcoin, the Bitcoin network was heavily bloated, so that the cost per transaction rose to absurd heights. This occurred because transaction fees are not fixed but based on supply and demand. They can therefore become quite expensive if demand gets too high. Although the network has been significantly improved since then, similar things could happen again during the next boom.

The number of technically possible transactions in the Bitcoin network is currently only about five to seven per second, which is far too little for a mass market. By comparison, credit card networks like Visa or MasterCard can process several thousand transactions per second. On the Lightning Network, many more transactions are possible.

Bitcoin is Not Anonymous

The Lightning Network can also remedy another weakness of Bitcoin: Bitcoin is not as anonymous as one might think. All transactions are stored in the Blockchain, publicly accessible to everyone. Although no real names are used, but only the cryptic Bitcoin addresses, these are far from being anonymous. If you publish a Bitcoin address on your blog or send it in an unencrypted email, everyone can see that this address belongs to you. One can then use a block explorer to see which transactions have been made using this address and how much money it contains.

Therefore it is highly recommended to use a new address for each transaction. If you were to use just one address, everyone could see how many Bitcoins you have, including the tax office, the mafia and other criminals. But even if you take this precaution, with a certain amount of computational effort one can still find out certain patterns of behaviour and transaction paths. This is contrary to the totally anonymous quality one should expect from cash.

The lack of anonymity is a major disadvantage of the current Bitcoin version. Competitors such as *Monero*, *Z-Cash* or *Horizen* place particular emphasis on privacy protection in order to differentiate themselves from Bitcoin. They use sophisticated encryption techniques for it and are therefore currently ahead of Bitcoin in terms of privacy.

However, with the Lightning Network Bitcoin can compensate for this disadvantage, as it works with a method called *Onion Routing*. Like onion skins, the individual nodes of the route are nested into each other and encrypted in the process. Thereofr, each node of the network can only recognise the previous node and the next node to which it is forwarding the payment. All others stations are encrypted. Neither the original sender nor the final recipient is known. Concerns about protecting your privacy on the Bitcoin network will therefore soon be a thing of the past.

Bitcoin is Too Volatile

For many people, the wild price fluctuations of Bitcoins, also called volatility, are a problem. Bitcoin's price has risen sharply over the years, but it has also experienced periods of large losses. Price jumps of 20 to 30% in one day have been seen both up and down. If you are not used to Bitcoin's volatility, you can easily get nervous, for example, when the 1000 euros you just received in Bitcoin are suddenly only worth 800 euros. Those who have experienced that a Bitcoin payment of 1,000 euros may rise to a value of 2,000 euros or more are probably less upset about it, but Bitcoin is certainly not for people with weak nerves.

For traders speculating on Bitcoin, its high volatility is great. If they have the intuition, they can make a lot of

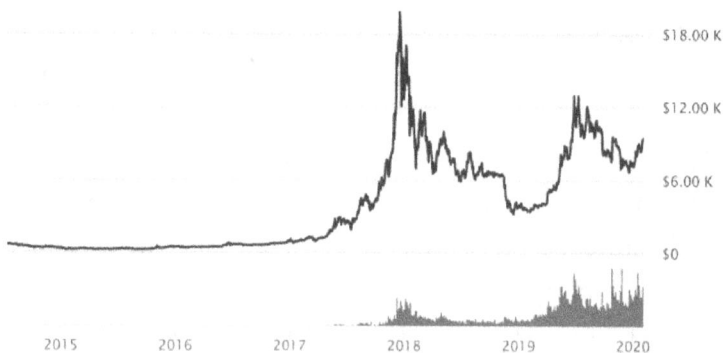

Bitcoin's price is very volatile

money, regardless of whether the price is going up or down. However, the strong fluctuations are rather unfavourable for everyday use. So far, it has been customary among Bitcoin users to make agreements on prices in euros or dollars and then use the respective daily exchange rate of Bitcoin for payment. However, an important function of money, namely to be a unit of account in which values are expressed, is currently not provided by Bitcoin.

3.6 Stable Coins

Many companies are therefore currently working on so-called *stable coins* with significantly less volatility. Some link their coin to fiat money, such as *Tether* or the *TrueUSD*. In the case of Tether, the issuing company originally promised to deposit one US dollar in a bank account for each Tether coin it generated. You could supposedly exchange your Tether for US dollars at any time. At present, there are about 9 billion Tether in circulation, which should be covered by 9 billion US dollars.

There were some doubts whether this was really true. Are the US Dollars really fully available, or does Tether operate a fractional reserve system? This would be possible because not all customers would want to redeem their Tethers at the same time. After some trouble with US regulators and much criticism within the Bitcoin community, Tether has moved away from the promise of full coverage.[9]

But regardless of whether this company can be considered trustworthy, such a pegging of a cryptocurrency to fiat money is a contradiction in terms. It is certainly not a solution for the imminent collapse of the monetary system. Other stable coins, such as the *Digix Gold Token* or the *Dinar Dirham* are allegedly backed by gold. But similarly, it is uncertain whether the issuing companies really have enough gold in their vaults. Again, you have trust one company, which is contrary to the original principle of Bitcoin, which is trustlessness.

Projects such as *DAI*, *Synthetix* or *Money-on-Chain* take a different approach. Here, cryptocurrencies are deposited as security. Nobody has to trust the issuing company, because cryptocurrencies are transparent and their Blockchains are publicly visible. While DAI and Synthetix are built on Ethereum, Money-on-Chain is based on Bitcoin, which is still by far the most secure and reliable cryptocurrency. Its Dollar-on-Chain is also pegged to the value of the US Dollar, but it is not backed by dollars but by Bitcoins. The dollar is merely a calculation unit that is used because people are familiar with it. Real dollars do not appear anywhere in the Money-on-Chain system.

Bitcoin owners can put their Bitcoins up as collateral and receive interest on them. These are paid by speculators who borrow the Bitcoins in order to bet on a rising or falling Bitcoin price. If they use not only their own coins but also the borrowed ones (which is called *Leverage*), their

Catalina Castro explains Money-on-Chain

chances of winning are much higher, even after having paid the interest for the owners of the Bitcoins. The speculators can make high profits if they have the right instinct, but can also lose a lot. Similar to a futures contract, the speculators take the risk and thus keep the DoC price stable. The less risk-taking owners of the DoC stable coin can be sure that it will not lose value, but in return they do not benefit from any price increases of the underlying Bitcoin.

Money-on-Chain is a clever concept because it retains the advantages of Bitcoin while producing stable currency units that people are familiar with. I can imagine that a stable coin such as the Dollar-on-Chain will take over the function as a means of payment in everyday life. Bitcoin, on the other hand, could act as an underlying reserve currency, a kind of "digital gold". In the future there will also be Euro-on-Chain, Yuan-on-Chain and other stable coins backed by Bitcoin, which work with the currently known currencies without being dependent on central banks. In the same way that, after the introduction of the Euro, people used to convert all amounts into the familiar lira, franc or peseta in their heads, the dollar, euro or yuan will certainly continue to live on in people's minds for some time, even if these currencies no longer exist or have become worthless due to hyperinflation.

I think the Money-on-Chain team's decision to go for Bitcoin is the right one because the Bitcoin Blockchain is by far the safest and most secure one in the world. I am in favour of free competition, and out of the many hundreds of Bitcoin clones, some definitely have their merits. But none of them has as high a chance of establishing itself as a world reserve currency and "new digital gold" as Bitcoin, and the reasons are as follows.

Only the Bitcoin network could be built up almost unnoticed by the public for several years, which gave Bitcoin an enormous competitive advantage. All of Bitcoin's competitors have been under close observation from the very beginning. Every software error, every wrong decision, every pre-mining into the pockets of the founders is commented on with malice and can lead to a price collapse. No one can take this first-mover-advantage away from Bitcoin anymore. A first-mover-advantage is much more important with money, which depends very much on the network effect and the trust of its users, than with other products, where the second or third mover can certainly turn out to be the winner.

Another advantage of Bitcoin over all the other cryptocurrencies is that there is no central point of attack. It has no "ingenious inventor" who throws his principles overboard, and who can use his authority to push through questionable changes to the software, as practiced sometimes by "Ethereum Pope" Vitalik Buterin.

Bitcoin's inventor Satoshi Nakamoto has deliberately disappeared without a trace. Therefore there is no "infallible authority" at Bitcoin. The developers of the Bitcoin Core Team are subject to strict control by everyone else and have to work hard to earn their professional recognition time and time again. Changes to the code can only be implemented with great persuasion throughout the community. What at first sounds like a disadvantage is in fact a great advantage for Bitcoin: it is extremely difficult to be changed, because no one controls or dominates it.

Given the advantages described above, I think the disadvantages of Bitcoin are manageable. Many smart people are working on fixing its current weaknesses. So far, the Bitcoin developers have always succeeded to overcome technical hurdles and Bitcoin has performed astonishingly well for more than 11 years. So I would say that the risk of investing part of your savings in Bitcoin is quite calculable.

Bitcoin is definitely a good tool to protect your money from expropriation by the state apparatus, and probably even to increase your wealth. However, there can be no absolute security in the computer world, and "you shall not put all eggs in one basket", as the old saying goes. Therefore, you should also consider other forms of investments. This is what the following chapter is about.

4. Austrian Investing

The economists Ludwig von Mises, Friedrich August von Hayek and Eugen Böhm von Bawerk mentioned in Chapter 1 belong to a school of thought called the *Austrian* or *Vienna School*. Their insights are very helpful for a better understanding of the monetary system. Everything I have written in *1.2 – The Monetary* System is based on them. The Austrians have convincingly analysed monetary systems, the nature of interest and the causes of economic cycles. Austrian economists predicted the economic crises of 1929 and 2008, while both surprised many other "economic wise men". Anyone who wants to get ready for the coming crisis is therefore well advised to study the teachings of the Austrian School.

This is what we want to do in the following chapter, without becoming too theoretical. Our focus is on how to keep your money safe in times of crisis and even how to increase it. Steffen Krug from the *Institute for Austrian Asset Management*, with whom I cooperated for this chapter, is specialised in this.

4.1 The Austrian School of Economics

The Austrian or Vienna School of Economics originated, as the name suggests, in Vienna in the middle of the 19th century. Its founder was Carl Menger, Professor of Economics at the University of Vienna. Other important figures were Eugen Böhm von Bawerk, Luwdig von Mises and Friedrich August von Hayek. In Austria itself, it plays hardly any role today, after its leading figures had to flee from the National Socialists in the 1930s. Their findings are rarely taught at universities around the world anymore. Exceptions are the *Unversidad Francisco Marroquín* in Guatemala, the *Universidad Rey Juan Carlos* in Madrid and the *George Mason University* in Fairfax, Virginia. This is probably due to the fact that the Austrian School is against any government interference in the economy, which is of course not welcome at state-funded universities. Most economists today are paid by state authorities, universities or central banks. They have no use for economists who are critical of the government and its central banks.

Eugen Böhm von Bawerk on an Austrian banknote

The economic schools that dominate today try to depict the economy in the form of mathematical models. This is viewed critically by the Austrians. They do not find it convincing to assume a purely rationally acting *homo economicus*, whose behaviour fits in with the theories but cannot be observed in reality. For Austrians, it matters how human beings act in real life. One of the most important books by Ludwig von Mises, therefore bears the title *Human Action*.[1]

The Austrian School had almost been forgotten for some time, but it has regained popularity in recent years. This was due in particular to the US politician Ron Paul, a convinced "Austrian" who ran for the office of US president several times and was able to fascinate young people in particular.

Another important factor: Bitcoin. The cryptouser @Mattoshin wrote this on Twitter: "Bitcoin's greatest success was turning a generation that just wanted to order psychedelic drugs online into full-fledged Austrian economists".[2] This may be a bit exaggerated, but there is indeed a large overlap between crypto users and followers of the Austrian School. I guess that many people only began to think about what money actually is when they studied Bitcoin, and then came across the works of monetary theorists such as Mises, Hayek or Mises' student Murray Rothbard.

4.2 Mises' Theories of Money

Ludwig von Mises was undoubtedly one of the most influential personalities of the Austrian School. He was born in 1881 in what is now Lviv in Ukraine. It was then called Lemberg and belonged to the Austrian-Hungarian Empire. Mises studied and habilitated with Eugen Böhm von Bawerk at the University of Vienna, but never received a professorship in Austria because of his Jewish origins and his critical attitude towards the government. Instead, he directed a private seminar from which many well-known economists emerged, including the later Nobel Prize winner Friedrich August von Hayek. Mises and Hayek ran the *Austrian Institute for Business Cycle Research* from 1927 until Hayek went to England in 1931 to teach at the London School of Economics. In 1938 Mises had to flee from the National Socialists, first to Switzerland, then to the

Ludwig von Mises

USA. He lived and taught in New York until his death in 1973. Mises influenced many masterminds of the libertarian movement in the USA, such as Murray Rothbard, Lew Rockwell and Ron Paul. Today, numerous economic research institutes around the world are named after him.

The Regression Theorem

Mises refined Carl Menger's theory of money in his habilitation thesis *Theorie des Geldes und der Umlaufmittel* ("The Theory of Money and Credit") which was published in 1912. He explains how money comes to its value, a question that economists had previously had their teeth into. The logical problem: there is a demand for money because it has purchasing power, and it has purchasing power because there is a demand for it. Mises solved this circular argument by including the time factor: people trust in money today because it had purchasing power yesterday, and they trusted in it yesterday because it had purchasing power the day before. If you go back further and further in time, you come to the point where a commodity took on a monetary function for the first time. According to this *Regression Theorem*, only precious metals such as gold or silver can be regarded as real money. We leave aside commodity money used in the past, such as livestock, shells or arrowheads, because these goods largely lost their monetary function. Banknotes were originally nothing more than receipts which the owner could exchange for gold or silver. The money we use today, which is no longer backed by any tangible assets, is worthless and harmful in the opinion of Ludwig von Mises. He was therefore a fierce opponent of fiat money that central and commercial banks can produce out of thin air (see Section 1.2). Mises advocated for a gold standard without a fractional reserve, in which each banknote is fully backed by gold.

Business Cycles According to Mises

Another important contribution by Ludwig von Mises to economics is his theory of business cycles. According to Mises, the main causes of extreme economic fluctuations are the central banks and their policy of artificially created money. In a truly free market, only money saved by reducing consumption can be used for investments. In a free market, interest rates are defined by supply and demand and thus have an important signal function: if a lot of saved money is available, the interest rate is lower; if less is saved, the interest rate is higher and investments are correspondingly more expensive.

In a centralised monetary system the interest rate is set arbitrarily by the central bank and thus loses its signalling and control function. In a free market, investors would only put their savings into projects for which there is a real need. But if money can be generated from nothing and pumped into the economy, the process is distorted. Cheap loans make otherwise senseless investments appear lucrative. This wastes resources and damages the economy in the long run. Sooner or later, an economic boom artificially created in this way will collapse and lead to painful corrections or even depression.

This was particularly evident in the world economic crisis of 1929. Since the *Federal Reserve System* of the USA was founded in 1913, it has provided the economy with low-interest loans, not only in the USA, but also in other countries. This led to an economic boom and a strong growth in share prices. When this bubble burst in the autumn of 1929, the adjustment of the economy to reality was painful but, according to Austrian Economics, unavoidable.

Murray Rothbard, a student of Mises, analysed the causes of the Great Depression in his book *America's Great Depression* of 1963.[3] He concluded that it was the countermeasures of politicians who wanted to fight unemployment with government stimulus programmes ("New Deal"), which turned a necessary corrective process into the Great Depression of the 1930s.

In his major work *Human Action*, Mises writes: "The wave-like movement affecting the economic system, the recurrence of periods of boom which are followed by periods of depression, is the unavoidable outcome of the attempts, repeated again and again, to lower the gross market rate of interest by means of credit expansion. There is no means of avoiding the final collapse of a boom brought about by credit expansion. The alternative is only whether the crisis should come sooner as the result of a voluntary abandonment of further credit expansion, or later as a final and total catastrophe of the currency system involved."[4]

4.3 The Austrian Portfolio

Although the Austrian School has existed for over 170 years, an investment strategy based on its teachings is still a relatively new phenomenon. For a long time, adherents of Austrian economics who wanted to invest money mostly followed the strategy of *Value Investing*. It was developed in the 1930s by Benjamin Graham and David Dodd and relates primarily to stocks and corporate bonds. The value of a company is measured by certain key figures, such as the price-earnings ratio, the debt-equity ratio, past earn-

Steffen Krug

ings power or dividend yield. The goal of value investors is to invest in undervalued companies and to profit from the market's recognition of their true value and corresponding increase in market price. One of the best-known representatives of this investment philosophy is Warren Buffett of *Berkshire Hathaway*, who is known for only investing in companies whose business he himself understands.

The first to create an investment strategy explicitly based on the teachings of the Austrian School has been Steffen Krug, the founder of the *Institute for Austrian Asset Management*, based in Hamburg, Germany. This chapter builds on his expertise. After studying economics in Heidelberg, Reims and Frankfurt (Oder) with some of the few professors who still belonged to the Austrian School, he worked for some time as a securities specialist for a bank and in 2001 became a self-employed investment consultant.

"With the onset of the global economic crisis from 2007 onwards, stock market prices were so inflated by the activities of the central banks that the value ratios reflected a distorted company valuation," says Steffen Krug. "For experts in Austrian monetary and economic theory, the 60% slump in value funds such as *Templeton Growth* at the beginning of 2009 was therefore no surprise. If you sit at a table with cheats who, like a central bank, can pull marked cards out of their sleeves, you have to change your strategy and can no longer rely on the old rules of the game".[5]

To his surprise, even after extensive research, he could not find an investment strategy based on Austrian principles anywhere in the world, so he decided to develop one himself. In the following we will present the main features of this strategy.

Physical Gold and Silver

Steffen Krug recommends to invest 30% of your assets in precious metals such as gold and silver – not in "paper gold" such as certificates or ETFs, but in real metal. You should store it in a bonded warehouse in Switzerland that is theft-proof. Of course, there is no such thing as 100% security, but Switzerland probably has the highest reputation in the world when it comes to the secure management of assets. With your storage certificate you can cross borders without fear of your gold being confiscated. The

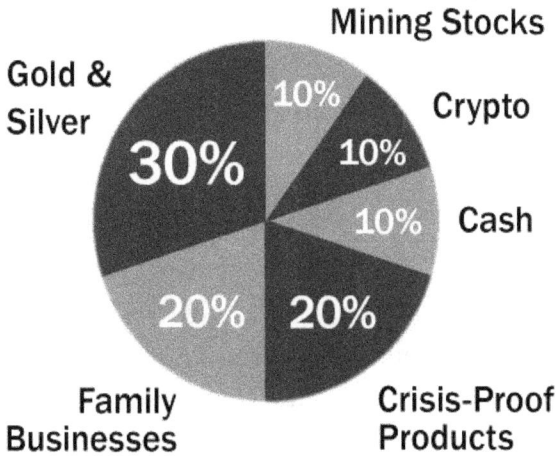

Steffen Krug's Austrian investment portfolio

disadvantage of precious metals is that they do not yield dividends or interest, and their storage costs money. In times of crisis, however, gold and silver will most likely see high price gains.

Stocks of Mining Companies

Investing in companies that mine gold, silver or other precious metals such as platinum can also lead to high price gains in times of crisis. In contrast to physical gold, you must take a close look at the key figures here, because you want to invest in a well-managed company. The advantage: if you buy a company's bond, you receive interest in addition to any price gains. If you buy shares, the company will hopefully pay dividends to its shareholders. The dividend yield of the last few years is therefore a value you should pay attention to. According to Steffen Krug you should invest 10% of your wealth in stocks of mining companies.

Shares and Bonds of Solid Family Businesses

Experience has shown that family businesses are better managed than those with an employed management team. While the latter are more focused on quarterly figures, family businesses tend to see the longer-term perspective. Entrepreneurs have "skin in the game"; they risk their personal fortunes and will always put first the long-term well-being of the company as a whole. Employed managers naturally do not do this; they tend to be short-term oriented and more interested in their next bonus payments than in preserving the capital substance of the company. Especially in times of crisis, you are therefore better advised to invest in solid, conservatively managed family businesses than in the latest start-ups from Silicon Valley. The recommended weighting for solid family businesses in the portfolio is 20%.

Companies that Make Crisis-Proof Products

Steffen Krug also recommends investing in companies whose products are in demand even in times of crisis. Luxury products, travel companies or restaurant chains are therefore to be ruled out, because most people will dispend with these things first. It makes more sense to invest in basic foods, cosmetics for daily use and energy. Warren Buffet is known for investing in stocks like Coca-Cola, Johnson & Johnson or General Electric.

"Nowadays, access to the Internet and to their mobile phones is essential for people," says Steffen Krug. "Internet providers and mobile phone companies are now fulfilling a basic need, so they fit into this category. Manufacturers of diesel generators could also be interesting, because people want to be able to charge their mobile phones even if the general power supply fails."[6] 20% of your portfolio should be invested in this type of company.

Cash

Steffen Krug recommends holding 10% of your portfolio in currencies that will still exist after the collapse of the Euro, for example the US dollar, the Singapore dollar, the Swiss franc or the Norwegian crown. An investment in fiat money may sound somewhat contradictory, after we did not talk about it very positively in the previous chapters. However, we are not talking about implementing the pure Austrian doctrine, but about surviving a period of crisis. Liquidity in cash is important for this, because what good are the best stocks and gold bars if you have to buy food? The US Dollar in particular will continue to play an important role as long as Saudi Arabia and the other

OPEC states only accept US dollars for their oil, a deal that US President Nixon negotiated with the Saudis in the 1970s in return for military protection. The USA is probably the only country in the world that can continue to run up debt and print money without restraint, because the Dollar will still be in demand worldwide for oil trading.

It is uncertain, however, how long the dollar will remain the world currency. None of the previous world currencies, neither the Spanish *Peso de Ocho* nor the British Pound, has been able to maintain its dominant position for more than a few hundred years. But for the near future, an investment in the US Dollar is still a good idea.

Crypto Currencies

According to Steffen Krug, 10% of your portfolio should consist of cryptocurrencies such as Bitcoin. This is a surprisingly high figure when you consider that his customer base consists less of computer nerds, but rather of elderly gentlemen dressed in suits and ties. "We already had a Bitcoin expert as a guest at our libertarian regulars' meetup in Hamburg in 2010," says Steffen. "Later, many people probably regretted not taking up his offer to buy Bitcoins from him – the price was less than a dollar at the time."[7] Steffen has also invited me twice to his investor conference to talk about Bitcoin, and the interest of the audience was surprisingly high.

The opinions of Austrian economists about Bitcoin are divided. Some of its representatives, such as Steffen Krug or Prof. Thorsten Polleit, President of the Mises Institute Germany, see Bitcoin as a welcome alternative to the Fiat money system. Other "Austrians", such as the US American Peter Schiff, who became popular through his easy-to-understand books on economic topics, are critical of Bitcoin. They see a contradiction to Mises' *Regression Theorem* (see Section 4.2), because Bitcoin, unlike gold or silver, was never a commodity that could be used for anything other than payment. Prof. Thorsten Polleit, president of the German Ludwig von Mises Institute argues that Bitcoin was created in a world where money already existed. People voluntarily exchange it for dollars, euros or other fiat currencies, whose value can be traced back to commodity money like gold or silver, if you go back further and further in time. This is how the apparent contradiction to the regression theorem can be resolved.[8]

Whether you follow the advice of Steffen Krug or you prefer to put together your own portfolio mix is, of course, up to you. Personally, I would give Bitcoin and other cryptocurrencies a higher weighting, because there is no other asset class with such high growth potential. A very practical service to trade gold against Bitcoin and thus hedge against strong fluctuations is *Vaultoro*. You can buy gold for Bitcoin there and exchange it back (but not the other way around). Vaultoro stores your gold in a Swiss bonded warehouse and it stays your personal property. If the Bitcoin price once again skyrockets and its next drop in price is foreseeable, you could exchange some of your Bitcoins for gold. When the Bitcoin price has fallen again, you can turn your gold back into Bitcoin and make high profits, if the price goes up again. If you had exchanged your Bitcoins for gold at the peak of the Bitcoin boom in 2017 at a rate near $20,000, you could have bought Bitcoins at the low point at the end of 2018 at a rate of $3500 with your gold. Although I expect less volatility in Bitcoin in the future, extreme price fluctuations will continue to occur, therefore a service that hedges these fluctuations with gold is very useful.

4.4 Weaknesses of Austrian Investing

Steffen Krug's recommendations are aimed at preserving long-term values and surviving a collapse of the financial system. One must be aware that there may then be phases in which the portfolio performs worse than other ones. The insights of the Austrian School might make you rather pessimistic about future developments, which might lead you to miss profit opportunities during the boom phase.

The Austrian economist William Anderson, professor at Frostburg State University, warned already in the summer of 1999 that the dot-com boom at that time was a bubble and would crash badly. That turned out to be completely correct. However, the price of the Nasdaq index at that time had not even reached half of its April 2000 peak. So anyone who followed Anderson's warnings in the summer of 1999 would miss out on the strongest phase of the boom.[9] It would have been more profitable to go along with the hype for a while, put some of your money into high-risk Internet stocks, pocket the profits and switch to an Austrian investment strategy in April 2000. However, this requires strong nerves and a good instinct for the right moment to exit.

Something similar happened with the subprime bust that triggered the financial crisis in 2007/2008. Mark Thornton, Senior Fellow at the Ludwig von Mises Institute in Alabama, had warned as early as 2004 that the boom would end in a major crisis and that banks would have to be rescued with taxpayers' money. At the time, the mainstream economists and the financial press smiled pityingly at this warning, but hardly anyone believed in it. And indeed, for about three more years a lot of money could be made with the derivatives that later triggered the crash. Stock market prices also continued to develop magnificently.[10] As long as the boom is still in full swing, those who foresee the bust may look like losers, although they will be right in the end.

As an Austrian style investor, you need patience and endurance. You could also adapt your investment strategy to the market situation: in boom times, you go with the flow and invest in every kind of nonsense that is in vogue.

When the bust phase starts, you sell everything and switch to an Austrian investment strategy as described before.

Are these investment tips enough to survive a crisis? I do not think so. After all, it's not just a question of putting your money in a safe place, but also of leading a good and safe life in general. This is what we want to deal with in the next two chapters.

5. Get Out of Tax Hell!

When the crisis comes, highly taxed countries such as Germany, Austria or Sweden will be hit particularly hard. People there are used to relying on a welfare state. Genuine human solidarity has been consistently diminished. After all, everyone pays a huge amount of taxes and expects something in return. Social structures such as families, religious communities, neighbourhoods or circles of friends, which served for thousands of years to provide social security, have largely been replaced by "Father State", as the Germans say without any irony. But this word monster shows that the welfare state educates its citizens to remain children. If the "father" becomes mortally ill, his children will get into serious trouble.

A great danger in the wealthy welfare states of Western Europe is the perception that they are so rich that things cannot end badly. But pride comes before a fall, as the saying goes. A good example is Venezuela. It shows that even the richest country in Latin America, which has the largest proven oil reserves in the world, can be ruined by Socialist policies.

Those who cannot imagine leaving their home countries at all can skip the following chapter. But those who are interested to start a business or a new life in a new place will find inspiration and practical tips in it. For this chapter I have cooperated with Christoph Heuermann, who advises people on how and where best to start a business, open a bank account or find a new place of residence. Christoph leads an unusual life. He is constantly on the move because his goal is to have visited all 193 UN member states at the age of 30, of which 150 he has already marked off.

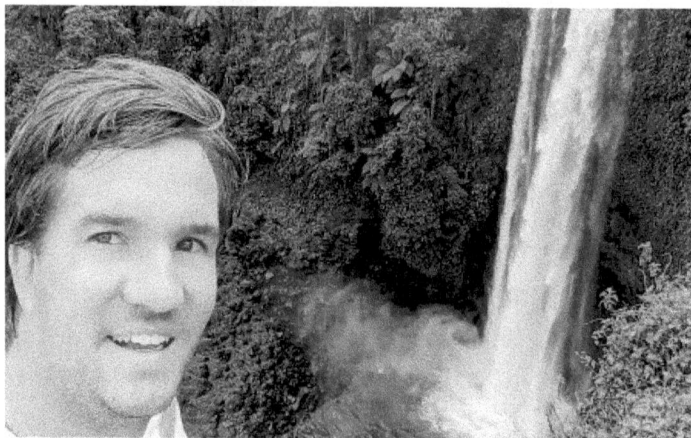

Christoph Heuermann, Perpetual Traveller

In 2019 alone, he visited 69 countries and, if you add up the kilometres, he has flown around the world more than four and a half times.[1]

But he does not do this just for fun. In every country he researches whether the living conditions there are favourable for immigrants and start-up founders. Over time, he has built up a worldwide network of local law firms and tax advisors who provide him with up-to-date information and put his recommendations into practice. His most important medium is the blog tax-free.today, which is also available in German, Spanish and French. Furthermore he publishes e-books and videos that deepen the blog's articles. He cleverly markets his adventurous life through social media and a personal travel blog to attract new customers for his products and consulting services. German television has also reported on him.[2]

Apparently Christoph Heuermann has struck a chord with his activities. His business is doing extremely well, so he can afford his numerous trips, and additionally invest in real estate, cryptocurrencies and agricultural land.

5.1 Reasons to Emigrate

As a German, I am most familiar with the situation in the country where I grew up, so in the following I will use Germany as an example. However, the problems described here can also be observed in other prosperous Western countries.

The West German economic miracle of the 1950s was essentially based on the free-market-friendly policies of Ludwig Erhard, who was for many years Minister of Economics and later Chancellor, the equivalent of Prime Minister in Germany. He was a member of the *Mont Pélérin Society*, founded by Friedrich August von Hayek, also Ludwig von Mises occasionally attended its meetings. These masterminds of the Austrian School were thus certainly close to him in matters of economic policy.

While the *Social Market Economy* he propagated is misunderstood by many as a combination of Socialism and the free-market, Erhard had a very different idea about it. For him *free* and *social* were synonymous when it comes to economic principles. In his view, the freer an economic order is, the more social it becomes. He was therefore a strict opponent of state interference in the economy, apart from a few regulatory measures such as cartel law. Erhard is quoted: "Nothing is generally more anti-social than the so-called welfare state, which reduces human responsibility and individual performance."[3]

But in the course of time Germany developed further away from Erhard's ideals. The "Socialists of all parties"[4] became more and more dominant over supporters of the free market. The libertarian author Roland Baader describes the current state of Germany as follows: "A socio-economic entity with a state education system, state health care and state pension system, with a state share of over 50% of the national product, with state-controlled agricultural markets, state-linked labour markets, state controlled fiat money and a corporatist functionary autocracy."[5]

In Germany today, out of a population of around 82 million, only 27 million people pay more in taxes than they take from the system through various social benefits. Of these, 12 million work for the federal, state or local governments, which means that they are financed by the tax money of the remaining 15 million.[6] It is easy to imagine how vulnerable such a system will be in the long run; especially since many of those still working productively today will retire in the next few years. The immigration of more than 2 million people from Africa and the Middle East since 2015, most of which will remain dependent on social benefits for the foreseeable future, is also not doing this system much good.

The tax burden on the productive fifth of the population, which has to feed the rest, is increasing. Today, the top tax rate in Germany already applies to those who earn 1.9 times the average income – in 1965, top taxpayers had to earn 15 times as much.[7] The costs and bureaucratic hurdles for entrepreneurs are becoming higher and higher. So it is no wonder that more and more Germans are thinking of emigrating.

Since Chancellor Merkel opened the German borders for economic migrants, the number of German emigrants has risen dramatically. Whereas in 2015 it was 138,237, in 2016 it more than doubled to 281,411. In 2017 and 2018 the number of German emigrants remained similarly high at 249,181 and 261,851 respectively. For comparison: in 1991 only 98,915 Germans left the country permanently.[8] Christoph Heuermann can confirm this trend. For some time now, his *Stateless* consulting service has been seeing a flood of inquiries, especially from Germany.

5.2 The Flag Theory

Even in our age of globalisation, many people still assume that they will spend their entire lives in the country where they were born and grew up. When they want to set up a business, open a bank account or invest money, nothing else comes to their mind but doing it in that one country. It is a generally accepted rule among investors that you "don't put all your eggs in one basket", i.e. you should spread your risk wisely. But when it comes to their own lives, this advice is mostly ignored. People place themselves under the control of the ruling elite in their own countries and thus take a high risk, especially in times of crisis. Even if you live in a relatively free country, it may not stay that way forever. It is therefore worthwhile to diversify your own life and make it crisis-proof.

Place your flags in many countries

"Planting flags in as many countries as possible maximises your freedom," recommends Christoph Heuermann. "Just as you would not put your wealth into a single stock, you should not rely on one country alone."[9]

The *Flag Theory*[10] on which Christopher's advice is based, was developed by the US investment guru Harry D. Schultz, who was at times listed by the Guinness Book of Records as the world's best-paid investment advisor. In his book *How to Keep Your Money and Your Freedom*[11] published in 1964, he originally referred to it as the *Three Flag Theory*. It is based on these three central principles:

1. Have your residence where foreign income is not taxed.
2. Have your businesses and assets in stable tax havens.
3. Live as a tourist in a country where you can be left alone.

By flags we do not mean national flags, but those small flag-shaped pins that are used to mark company locations or previous travel destinations on a world map. You might put a flag on the country of which you are a citizen, a flag on the one where you run your business and a flag on the one where you actually live. The important thing is that these are three different countries. Of course, you can have businesses and residences in more than one country, and you can also distribute your flags around the globe for other purposes, such as asset management. That is why the *Three Flag Theory* has been renamed *Flag Theory*.

Let's take Christoph Heuermann himself as an example: he has a German passport (flag 1) with which he can travel visa-free to many countries and obtain required visas relatively easily. He is not registered in Germany anymore, and as he stays there for less than 183 days a year he is not taxable under German law. His official permanent residence is in Panama (flag 2). There he only pays taxes on money earned in Panama, but has a legal tax rate of 0% on all income generated outside the country. He does not have to stay permanently in Panama for this. His company, through which the consultations and sales of books and videos are conducted, is registered in Florida, where the corporate tax rate for non-resident foreigners is 0% (flag 3). He also holds equity in companies in Georgia and Austria (flags 4 and 5).

Of course, Christopher's extreme lifestyle is not everyone's cup of tea, but it is not necessary to follow his example. Often it is enough to think a bit outside the box and study the tax and company laws of other countries. You quickly realise that you do not have to be a large corporation or a super-rich person to escape a tax hell like Germany, Austria or Sweden. You just have to put your flags on countries where you are treated better. A model consisting of only two or three countries is already sufficient to take advantage of many benefits.

5.3 Models of Taxation

Let's have a look at how countries deal with taxation, especially income tax. The following models exist:

No Income Tax

There are 23 countries in the world that do not levy income tax at all. These include rich oil states like Kuwait, Qatar or the United Arab Emirates, which make so much money from their oil revenues that they do not need any taxes. Some small states such as the Cayman Islands or the British Virgin Islands have a different strategy. They deliberately waive income and corporate taxes to attract companies of the financial sector, such as hedge funds.

In both cases, however, it is difficult to obtain a residence permit in those countries, so they are not really suitable for emigrants. Quite well known as a tax haven is Monaco on the Cote d'Azur, which does not levy income tax, except for French citizens. The catch: you need to have at least half a million euros on your bank account in order to be allowed to settle in Monaco. Also the real estate prices are so high that Monaco as a place of residence can only be considered by millionaires. Other states on this list of 23 are very insecure and unattractive, as for example Somalia or Western Sahara.

Residence Principle

Almost all European countries and most countries in the world apply the residence principle. This means: if you live in a state, you have to pay tax on all your worldwide income there. With few exceptions, the 183-day rule applies: if you spend less time than that in a country, you are not taxable there. Furthermore, it is important that there are no other signs of a "centre of life". In countries with a registration obligation, such as Germany or Austria, it is therefore necessary to de-register from the Citizens' Registration Office. Rental contracts, gym memberships and other obligations that indicate that you live in this country should be terminated. If you own a condominium, it should be rented out on a long-term basis. The tennis millionaire Boris Becker, who had left Germany and registered in Monaco, possessed a key to an apartment in Munich which he officially did not own. However, it was the reason why the German tax office regarded him as liable for tax in Germany and demanded several million euros from him.

Taxation by Citizenship

There are only two states in the world that require their citizens to file a tax return no matter where they live: Eritrea and the USA. Especially the US tax authorities mercilessly enforce this principle all around the world. As a US citizen, most of the advice given by Christoph Heuerman is therefore not applicable. The only option as a US citizen is to move to Puerto Rico, which belongs to the USA but is not a state in its own right and is therefore treated differently in terms of taxation. Other than moving to Puerto Rico, to stop paying US you would have to give up your US citizenship. For this alone, the USA charges a fee of over 2000 dollars.

Territorial Principle

Around 40 countries in the world apply the territorial principle, which means that they tax only the income that their inhabitants earn within the country, but not income earned outside. These countries are particularly interesting for emigrants. Among them are Panama, the Philippines,

Paraguay, Georgia, and Guatemala. These are mainly developing countries where one should take a close look at the general quality of life and the level of crime.

One of the few highly developed countries with a territorial principle is Hong Kong, but there the barriers to permanent immigration are very high. In addition, there are a number of countries that apply the residence principle for personal taxation, but the territorial principle for corporate taxation. These include Singapore, Algeria, Tunisia and Morocco.

In addition to income tax, there are other forms of tax, such as sales tax, VAT, property tax, etc. In some countries, high customs duties are levied on imported goods such as cars or computers, which makes these things very expensive. So you should not only look at income tax alone, but also at all other taxes and the associated cost of living.

You can achieve a lot by cleverly combining different flags. If you are a citizen of a country with residence taxation, you have already gained a lot by moving to a country with territorial taxation, especially if your business is global and your "new home country" is not an important market for your business.

5.4 From Panama to Prospera

In his book *Weil Dein Leben dir gehört* ("Because your life belongs to you") Christoph Heuermann describes the conditions for emigrants and entrepreneurs in 50 selected countries. I have chosen five of them as examples to give you an idea of what is possible. More detailed information can be found in Christophe's book and blog.

Panama

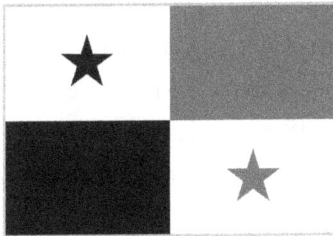

Panama is the southernmost country in Central America, bordering Costa Rica to the west and Colombia to the east. Panama was separated from Colombia in 1903 on the initiative of the USA so that the Panama Canal could be built there. This canal connects the Atlantic and Pacific Oceans and saves ships the long journey around Cape Hoorn. For a long time Panama was a kind of colony of the USA, which had full control over the Canal Zone until 1999. Therefore many of the approximately 4 million Panameños speak good English.

Because of the income from the canal fees and its role as a financial centre, Panama is today one of the richest countries in Latin America. The official currency is the

Balboa, which is pegged 1:1 to the US dollar. However, Balboa coins are only available up to the value of one dollar, so most of the payments in Panama are made directly in US dollars. Panama is considered relatively safe by Latin American standards. However, the cost of living is higher than in most other Latin American countries.

Panama uses the territorial taxation principle. Income earned outside the country is therefore tax-free. Income in Panama is only taxable if you stay there for at least 183 days per year. For individuals there is a tax allowance of 11,000 USD per year. Income up to 50,000 USD is taxed at 15%, higher incomes at 25%. The corporate income tax for companies is a uniform 25%. It is relatively easy to obtain a permanent residence permit and, in the long run, citizenship. For citizens of 48 countries, including all member states of the EU, it is possible to obtain a residence permit if

> 1. you have established a company in Panama (which need not be active)
>
> 2. you can prove a residence in Panama (the address of a hotel is sufficient).
>
> 3. you provide proof of financial independence by depositing at least 5000 US dollars in a Panamanian bank account.

In addition to the minimum bank balance the entire procedure will cost you approximately 5000 US dollars. A minimum yearly stay in Panama is, in contrast to many other countries, not necessary. It is sufficient to visit Panama every two years to keep your residence permit.

"This makes Panama ideal as a safe haven for all those who cannot or do not want to leave their home country yet, but are looking for a safe place for the future, or for those who tend to travel a lot but want to avoid the running costs of a permanent home," says Christoph Heuermann. He therefore considers Panama the ideal place of residence for permanent travellers.[12]

Five years after obtaining your residence permit, you may apply for full citizenship. The chances of getting it are better if you are invested in the country and have been there regularly.

Philippines

In the Pacific Ocean, southeast of China, lies the Republic of the Philippines. It consists of 7641 islands, of which 880 are inhabited. The largest is Luzon, where the capital Manila is located. About 23 million of the over 100 million Filipinos live there. From the 16th to the 20th century the Philippines were a Spanish colony, therefore Catholicism is the dominant religion. After the Spanish-American War of 1898 and the suppression of the Philippine independence movement, the Philippines became a colony of the United States. Since 1946, the Philippines have been independent, but the USA retained special economic rights for several decades. Today the US still operate several military bases and play an important role in Philippine politics. English is therefore now the second official language in the Philippines and its general language, more widely spoken than its official language, Filipino.

Residents are subject to tax on their worldwide income, but in the case of foreigners, only the portion earned in the Philippines is taxable. The tax rate for this is 5 to 32 %, depending on the amount of income. The Philippines offer a number of visa programmes that make it relatively easy to emigrate there. For example, if you invest USD 75,000, you can obtain an investor visa called SRIV. For investments in tourism projects, 50,000 US dollars is sufficient. By the age of 35, you can apply for a "pensioner" visa, for which you must prove regular income from abroad. Alternatively, you may pay a deposit of between 1,500 and 50,000 US dollars.

You may get your tourist visa, which is issued for 30 days upon arrival, extendable by a further 6 months at the Immigration Office. You can repeat this process several times without leaving the country. Only after three years it is recommended to leave and re-enter the country.

For Christoph Heuermann, the Philippines are the best destination in Asia: "As an emigrant with tax-free foreign income, you can live there perfectly well, even if you earn relatively little. The Philippines is therefore particularly suitable for people over 35 who want to set up an online business on the side. With 500 euros per month you can live a comfortable life."[13]

Paraguay

Paraguay is located in South America between Bolivia, Brazil and Argentina. It is a landlocked country without access to the ocean. Paraguay became independent from Spain in 1811, but after losing the Triple Alliance War against Brazil, Argentina and Uruguay (1864 to 1870), it had to cede about 50% of its territory to the victorious powers.

Paraguay operates the Itaipú hydroelectric power station together with Brazil, and the Yacyretá station with Argentina. These gigantic power stations supply considerably more electricity than the approximately 7 million Paraguayans can consume. Therefore Paraguay exports a large part to the neighbouring countries and its hydro electricity is an important source of income. Cheap electricity also makes Paraguay a popular location for Bitcoin mining.

For decades Paraguay has been supplying its neighbouring countries with cheap electronic goods, household goods and textiles from the Far East, especially through the border city Ciudad del Este. Paraguay is also the largest marijuana producer in South America.

The principle of territorial taxation applies to private individuals, so income generated outside the country is tax-free. Paraguay does not exactly sound like a paradise for emigrants otherwise, but it offers something that qualifies it as an attractive spot for one of your "flags". You can get an official residence permit of 10 years there relatively easily. All you have to do is make a deposit of about 4200 US dollars at the National Bank, which you can use freely after six months. In addition, you must submit a police clearance certificate. A stay in the country is not required for this.

The big advantage of Paraguay: It is a full member of *Mercosur*. This South American organisation has similar advantages to the EU, like freedom of travel for all citizens, but without imitating its disadvantages, such as excessive central bureaucracy. As a Paraguayan identity card holder, you can travel freely to all Mercosur member states, including full members Argentina, Brazil and Uruguay, as well as associated members Bolivia, Chile, Colombia, Ecuador and Peru (Venezuela was excluded in 2016).

Christoph therefore recommends to his clients to acquire a residence permit and identity card in Paraguay: "You can easily keep your previous citizenship, but with the Paraguayan identity card you have greater freedom of movement. Especially if a passport was to be revoked for whatever reason, one could enter South America with the ID card alone. So it is a very good crisis precaution."[14]

Georgia

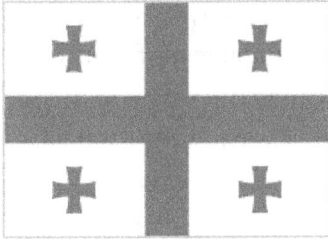

If you are from Europe and don't want your new residence more than 12 hours away by plane, Georgia is a good place to live. It is only a three to four hour flight from Central Europe and is served by several budget airlines. Located between the Black Sea and the Caucasus, the former Soviet Republic has become a paradise for entrepreneurs. Georgia has been an independent state since 1991, with the provinces of Abkhazia and South Ossetia having declared themselves independent through the help of Russia. The 3.7 million Georgians are predominantly Christian Orthodox. Georgia is famous for its excellent wines and cuisine, and this at a relatively low cost of living.

Georgia is the only European country with territorial taxation. Income within Georgia is taxed at 20%, income outside Georgia is tax-free. For companies, Georgia applies the same clever system as Estonia: a 15% tax is only due on dividend payments to shareholders. Profits that are reinvested in the company remain tax-free, even if they are generated in the country.

Already as a tourist you are not granted the usual 30 or 90 days stay, but you can spend a whole year in Georgia without any further formalities. You are even allowed to work there. A temporary residence permit, which you have to renew every six months, can be obtained if you set up a company in Georgia with an annual revenue of at least 17,000 euros. Alternatively, you can invest 300,000 euros in a Georgian business. If you purchase a property, a value of 100,000 euros is sufficient. You can apply for Georgian citizenship after five years.

Georgia offers good conditions for opening a private bank account. As a foreigner you only need a passport, but you must be present in person. Georgia is not a member of the SEPA zone, but it offers IBAN transactions to all participating countries at a relatively low cost. TBC Bank and the Bank of Georgia offer online banking in English and an international Visa card. You can manage your account not only in the local currency Lari, but also in Euro or Dollar. They even pay interest on your balance.

Another advantage of Georgia: there is no compulsory social security. If you hire employees, unlike almost all other European countries, there is no high percentage of social security contributions for entrepreneurs.

Despite the somewhat unstable political situation with neighbours such as Russia, Azerbaijan and Turkey, Christoph Heuermann warmly recommends Georgia: "Whether skiing in the Caucasus or swimming in the Black Sea – the Georgians impress with their hospitality and openness. A visit to this up-and-coming Caucasus country is therefore highly recommended for every perpetual traveller."[15]

Prospera

An interesting case is the city of Prospera, which is still under construction on the Caribbean island of Roatán. It is not an independent state, but a *Zona de Empleo y Desarollo Económico (ZEDE)*, or "Zone for Job Creation and Economic Development", as made possible under the law of its host country Honduras. It is a special zone that is still part of Honduras, but has its own legal system and administration. Prospera is run by a private company with whom the immigrant signs a contract with clearly defined rights and duties. In addition, there is also a ZEDE government which is supervised by the government of Honduras. Prospera is not a purely private city but a kind of public-private partnership with the state of Honduras. However, it does comes very close to the ideal of Titus Gebel, who formulates the concept of the *Free Private City* as follows:

"Imagine a private company as a service provider which offers you protection of life, freedom and property in a delimited area. This service includes security, a legal and regulatory framework and independent dispute resolution. You pay a contractually fixed amount per year for this. The service provider cannot unilaterally change the contract without your consent. You have the legal right to demand that it be complied with and a claim for damages in the event of poor performance."[16]

Titus Gebel, author of the book *Free Private Cities*, is an investor and board member of the company that is developing Prospera. He is also involved in similar projects that will be developed in Africa and the Caucasus.

For a fixed fee, the operating company provides things you would expect from a functioning state (not necessarily from Honduras): a non-corrupt police force, efficient courts, and a minimum level of infrastructure. You are not treated as a "subject" by the operating company, but as a customer. If, for example, the guaranteed security is breached and you are robbed, you can sue the operating company for damages – of course not at the courts it operates itself (those are for disputes among the residents), but at a higher, neutral level. For this purpose, private arbitration courts are used, as is common practise in international commercial law.

Christoph Heuermann has a financial stake in the operating company and plans to invest in real estate there. "What is needed on Roatán are mostly pioneers who identify with the idea of the Free Private City and want to help building it," he says "Prospera is an ideal new opportunity for people who are gifted in craftsmanship and for whom tax and regulatory freedom is otherwise rather difficult to achieve. Whether baker or cook, carpenter or architect – all are needed in Prospera and can realise their ideas."[17]

Immigration to Prospera is not yet possible, but you may apply for pioneer status probably by the end of 2020.

5.5 But Who Will Build the Roads?

Is it morally reprehensible to avoid paying taxes like Christoph Heuermann does by all legal means? I think the opposite is the case. Whoever takes another person's property away from him under threat of violence commits robbery. Whoever does this secretly commits theft. According to the principle of equal treatment, these crimes should be generally outlawed. But while ordinary citizens are punished for robbery or theft, the state does exactly the same thing without a punishment, which is not acceptable.

Robbery is referred to by the state as direct tax, for example in the form of income or corporate tax. If you refuse to give up your property you will be threatened with imprisonment, and if that does not scare you into compliance, with physical violence or death. For theft, the state uses terms such as value added tax, tobacco tax or luxury tax. Many consumers do not even notice this when they buy a product. Money is secretly taken out of their pockets, which does not benefit the supplier of the product as intended, but the state apparatus.

The State is a Gang of Robbers

"Take away justice – what else is a state other than a big gang of robbers?" goes a quote by St. Augustine. Pope Benedict XVI used this quote in his speech before the German parliament[18] – an absolute highlight in politics. Justice is constantly taken away when the state commits the property crimes it calls taxes. It is indeed behaving like a gang of robbers and thieves. Citizens have not only the right, but also the obligation to defend themselves against such criminal acts.

Of course, certain community tasks must be financed in some way. But is the state, as a monopolist without competitors, really in the best position to do this? Private providers could offer the vast majority of services currently provided by the state much more efficiently and cheaply in a free competition. The often cited roads are not built by the government, but by companies specialising in this task; only the financing is done by taxpayers' money. The roads could just as well be financed by a system of tolls for which only the actual users of the roads pay.

But what about education, healthcare and social security, which definitely are important issues? Experience shows that private educational and charitable institutions work much better than a monopolist, because they have to compete. Furthermore, in the state apparatus it is not the best experts who rule but those with the biggest egos, the right party memberships and the best connections. This usually leads to worse results. We should not leave important things such as education or healthcare to politicians, who usually are not experts in those fields, and whose main interest is to stay in power at the expense of others.

Fees Instead of Taxes

Even if we agree that some services, such as police, fire brigade or courts, should be in the hands of a central provider, taxes have proven to be the worst possible method of financing them. By definition, unlike fees, taxes are not dedicated to a specific purpose. A small group of people is given the power to decide over the property of others and of its disposal. However, they do not take any responsibility for the correct use of these funds, nor do they have to take any form of liability for the damage they do. It is in the nature of things that such a privilege leads to a wasteful use of funds. After all, it is other people's money, and if something goes wrong, you are not liable for it.

In today's majority voting system called "democracy", every political group tries to give its clientele more benefits to ensure their re-election, such as higher pensions, higher child benefits or stricter environmental laws. The problem is, that those who have to pay for all this are now in the minority and are regularly outvoted by the beneficiaries. Such a system, which punishes productive work and rewards laziness and irresponsible action, will not be able to survive in the long term.

The situation is quite different with fees for specific services, as is the case with Prospera. For your monthly payment, you will receive a detailed list of the services you can expect in return. The service provider cannot simply change the fee arbitrarily or offer a worse service; otherwise you would sue him for damages, demand your payment back and, if necessary, terminate the contract. However, you do not have a proper contract with your government, only the legendary *Contrat Social*, which no one has ever seen, let alone signed.

Any sensible person should strive to replace taxes with a better system of community funding. All payment flows should be transparent, and citizens should be able to decide for themselves what their money is used for. I describe such a model in Chapter 8. Those who support the current unfair and inefficient system are preventing a better one from taking hold. Christoph Heuermann and his services therefore fulfil an important social task.

6. Mastering the Crisis

It is difficult for us to imagine what our daily life would be like if a serious financial and economic crisis were to break out. The Corona crisis in early 2020 gave us a foretaste. Will there be supply bottlenecks and power cuts? Will there be civil war-like conditions with looting and rampant crime? Or will people in need move closer together and help each other?

For this chapter I have cooperated with Bettina Falck, who has been working on various crisis scenarios for some time. She is the founder and managing director of a strategic security agency that advises companies and private individuals on how to minimise their risk – and we are not talking about losses on the stock market, but real risks to life and health. Her company collects security and risk-related data worldwide and prepares it in such a way that particularly critical situations can be avoided from the outset. Its main customers are companies whose employees travel a lot in crisis areas around the world. Her service is also useful for banks and insurance companies as well as in the logistics and transport sectors. Insurance companies use her data for risk calculations and trend analyses.

"We create situation pictures of risks in an easily comprehensible form, for example in the form of event and topic-oriented maps," explains Bettina. "Recently, we have also been able to analyse data from social media and are therefore able to identify and publish crisis situations earlier than the conventional news agencies."[1]

Bettina Falck has written a book, which she calls *Instructions for Self-Assertion in the Matrix*. She gives numerous tips on how to to live a free and self-determined life.

"By *Matrix* I don't mean that we live in a large computer simulation," she says with a smile. "But as in the film of the same name, it's about recognising that reality is different from what the rulers want us to believe. The Matrix is what I call the bureaucratic-technocratic power apparatus, which is primarily interested in self-preservation. We are deluded into believing that we have freedom and democracy, but the reality is that we as individuals are subordinated to the rule of this power apparatus."[2]

Bettina Falck

Bettina kindly allowed me to use the 300-page manuscript of her book. Unfortunately, she is so busy building up her business that she has yet to publish it — I hope she will as it would certainly be of great benefit to many people.

6.1 Protect your Privacy!

Increasingly important as a preventive measure against future abuse is the protection of our privacy in the digital realm. Today we are constantly reachable or trackable through the GPS location function of our mobile phone at any time. Voluntarily or involuntarily we disclose a lot of information which can be used against us. Many people think: "I have nothing to hide, so what could happen?" But this is a very naive attitude. Criminals and government agencies can already learn many things about us through our tweets or Facebook and Instagram posts, which they can use to our disadvantage. Often we are not even aware of this. But who knows if the sympathetic democratic government of today will be replaced by a repressive dictatorial one tomorrow, or develop into one?

Imagine, for example, that one day the private ownership of gold will be banned, as it happened in the USA in 1933. If you spent a lot of time on gold websites before and ranted on Facebook about the manipulation of the gold price, it will be hard for you to convince the confiscation squad standing outside your door that there is nothing to be gained from you.

Or, you bought Bitcoins at a low price a few years ago and brag about your bargain in various online forums and Facebook groups. In doing so, you assume that one-year gains from Bitcoin transactions will remain tax-free, which corresponds to the current legal situation in Germany. But suddenly the law is changed, even retroactively. If you do not declare the Bitcoins in your next tax return, you will probably have a problem.

Criminals also use social media. If you constantly post pictures of what great cars you drive, how beautiful your home is and how cute your children are, you shouldn't be surprised if the cute child becomes a kidnap victim one day. Kidnappings are unfortunately very common in many countries of the world, and children are favourite victims. They are most precious to us and it is difficult to protect them around the clock. It is foreseeable that this most despicable type of crime will also become more common in Western countries.

Do you think these three scenarios are overly pessimistic? I think there could be many further negative ones. One thing is clear: In each of these cases, you could have avoided a lot of trouble by having been more discrete in social media. All-round surveillance was still a huge expense for the Soviet Union's secret police. It meant bugging apartments and paying hundreds of thousands of official and unofficial employees. Nowadays, much of surveillance can be automated and operated via the Internet, so that full surveillance can be obtained for as little as one US dollar a day.[3] Many people also make it unnecessarily easy for the surveillants. They post the most private things under their real name, even in conjunction with their phone number.

Incognito, Ergo Sum[4]

Bettina Falck therefore advises to remain as incognito as possible on the Internet, especially in social media such as Facebook, Twitter or Instagram. The best thing to do is not to use social media at all. If they are important for you professionally, you should really focus your social media communication on professional issues. If you cannot live without social media, it's best to get an alias that is not immediately recognisable as such. So instead of *CryptoMonster*, you should rather take *CindyMiller*. And, of course do not post pictures of your children or show off your wealth.

"It's all about maintaining a low profile, which means to not stand out from the crowd," explains Bettina Falck. "That doesn't mean to go completely underground, but you should offer as little exposure as possible. You can take an example from some of the richest people in Germany, whose companies almost everyone knows. But you know next to nothing about their founders."

Messenger services of the companies Apple and Facebook (the latter also runs the popular *WhatsApp*) are generally not recommended, as it is well known that these companies cooperate with the US intelligence agencies. Better, because fully encrypted, are *Telegram*, *Threema* or *Signal*. You can use them to send messages without Uncle Sam reading along.

Patterns of Behaviour

However, except in cases of concrete suspicion of a serious crime, intelligence agencies are not that interested in reading your conversations and texts. What they find much more useful is the metadata, which they receive automatically. These metadata provide much more valuable information for monitoring and controlling people. For example, the everyday mobility of most people is of an almost obsessive regularity. Many people spend most of their time in only a few places and generally move within a radius of between one and a maximum of ten kilometres from their centre of life. These patterns of behaviour are as individual as fingerprints.

This was shown by the analysis of movement profiles of tens of thousands of mobile phone users by scientists from Boston led by the Hungarian physicist Albert-Lász-ló Barabásivi. According to his findings, even with people who travel often and long distances, one can estimate with a probability of around 80 per cent when they will be where. In the case of people who travel little, their movement behaviour of the next few days can even be predicted with a probability of up to 93 per cent.

Recognising and predicting individual behaviour patterns is the basis of every crime, whether committed by private criminals or by the government. The only protection against this is to leave either false traces or non-recognisable patterns. Metadata, which can be read out from mobile phones and electronic payment transactions can be described and extrapolated to create these patterns. You should therefore either completely do without these technical aids or not use any SIM cards or credit cards registered in your name. Better alternatives are unregistered prepaid SIM cards and anonymous prepaid debit cards.

Encrypt Your Communication!

Another important privacy issue is encryption. You should only send and receive emails in encrypted form. This was quite cumbersome in the past, but now there are commercial providers such as Proton mail, Posteo or Tutanota, which are relatively easy to use. It is important that you not only encrypt emails with "sensitive" content, but all your emails without exception, otherwise attention would be drawn to the few encrypted ones.

For surfing the net Bettina Falck recommends a *Virtual Private Network (VPN),* and the service *TOR ("The Onion Router").* Both of them hide the traces you would otherwise leave behind when visiting websites. TOR is the only way to access the websites of the so-called Dark Web that cannot be found on the public World Wide Web. There you can buy things that are hard to find elsewhere, like psychedelic drugs or other things deemed "illegal".

Monero has emerged as the currency of the Dark Web, because this cryptocoin works much more anonymously than Bitcoin. You can exchange Monero for Bitcoin or other cryptocurrencies on a crypto exchange like Shapeshift or Changelly, or you can buy it for US dollars or euros on exchanges like Huobi, Binance or Bitfinex. Cryptocurrencies and analogue cash are preferable to credit and debit cards as a means of payment because they leave significantly fewer traces.

Incognito in the Real World

Even in the real world you should avoid any unnecessary disclosure of private data. For example, your name, address and telephone number do not belong in a publicly accessible telephone directory. You should also avoid writing your name on the doorbell and on your front door. In the case of detached houses, the house number is sufficient for the mail and visitors to reach you. For apartments in multi-family houses, it is sufficient to give an apartment number, as is customary in many countries of the world. And what to think of colourful signs in children's writings saying *"Bob, Alice, Liam and Emma Thompson live here"*? That is something I probably do not need to explain in view of my comments on child abductions.

Bitcoin guru Andreas Antonopoulos even goes so far as to give a false name when he is asked for it at Starbucks.[5] To have one's first name handwritten on a coffee cup for a few minutes is not particularly dangerous in my opinion, but Andreas acts out of principle. He is a radical advocate of privacy, and rightly so, because without privacy there is no freedom.

6.2 Be Prepared for an Emergency!

If many banks go bankrupt, this will have a considerable impact on the economy. Even economically healthy companies will then no longer be able to obtain loans. Supermarkets will no longer be able to pay their suppliers and the highly complex supply chains that make life in cities possible will be interrupted. Another very realistic crisis scenario is a power failure lasting several days.

In Germany for example, such a scenario is very likely due to the shutdown of functioning power plants and the prioritisation of renewable energies, which are less reliable than conventional energy sources. On days with little wind and sunshine, Germany has on several occasions only just missed a total blackout of the power grid. By purchasing electricity from neighbouring countries for higher prices, the energy companies avoided blackouts. But this is something you cannot rely on, especially not in times of crisis. Without electricity, hardly anything works in our highly technological world. Traffic lights and public transport are out of order, food rots on the refrigerated shelves of supermarkets and in the wholesalers' cold stores, and it is likely to become difficult to supply the most essential necessities.

If you do not live on a farm but in a city, which depends on supplies from outside, you should stock up on emergency supplies for such particularly critical times. You don't have to become a "Doomsday Prepper" for that. Preppers (from the Boy Scout motto "Be Prepared") or Survivalists are people who prepare for survival in the event of a disaster. They store supplies, tools and weapons, and even hold military exercises in case of a civil war. This can sometimes seem a bit sectarian, but that should not discourage you. The idea of being prepared for an emergency is absolutely correct; that doesn't mean you are eager for it. Rather think of the jack in your car that you hopefully never need. Or the umbrella which seems to have the magical effect of preventing rain when you carry it with you, only to allow the rain on days you left it at home.

It is by no means just a few crazy survivors stockpiling supplies for emergencies. The *German Federal Office for Civil Protection and Disaster Relief* also advises that emergency supplies should always be kept in the house for at least ten days.[6] You can buy special emergency food for this purpose, which is long lasting, takes up little space and contains all the essential nutrients that humans need. Also well suited are the so-called EPAs, each containing a daily ration for one person.

You should better not post on Facebook when your bulk pack of emergency food arrives, even if you can hardly resist shooting a cool selfie with it. In an emergency, you could be the only well-prepared person in your neighbourhood, and thus a target for hungry looters. So, order your emergency supplies in small quantities one-by-one and store them discreetly. You can also bury them in your garden if you have one and there is not enough space in your home. The most important thing is to have enough drinking water in the house, in case the water supply breaks down, because without water people can only survive for a short time. For this purpose, water purification tablets are also useful to make dirty water from ponds and rivers drinkable.

The most important medicines should not be missing from your emergency supply. Start first with those that you have to take regularly or need for survival, as well as cold remedies, painkillers and antipyretics, remedies for gastrointestinal diseases, electrolytes, clinical thermometers, splinter tweezers, disinfectants and bandages.

"What many people don't think about: if there's no electricity, after a while the toilets don't work either, because the water for flushing is pumped up with electric pumps," explains Bettina. "The most important emergency supplies therefore include chemicals such as those used in portable or camping toilets."[7]

You should also always have enough cash in small bills in the house, because in case of a financial crisis, banks and ATMs will certainly be closed for a long time. The amount of cash you can withdraw from your account will probably be strictly limited. The Cypriots and Greeks have only recently experienced this. And ATMs do not work during a power outage anyway.

It is advisable to pack an "escape backpack" or "go-bag" in case you have to leave the house in a hurry. Bettina Falck recommends the following contents for this:

- waterproof document bag with officially certified copies of important documents (birth certificate, passport or identity card, driving licence, diploma)
- memory card (mini SD card, better: micro SD with at least 16 GB plus SD adapter) or USB stick with all important files in encrypted form
- emergency radio, at least AM/FM/KW, possibly with solar charging technology and/or crank dynamo operation (as well as USB slot for charging the mobile phone)
- optional: CB handheld radio
- LED flashlight, robust, high light output, possibly with signal functions and stroboscope
- reserve batteries and/or accumulators
- aluminium-coated emergency blanket
- light-, dirt-, water- and wind-resistant trekking jacket with minimal packing volume/emergency poncho
- first aid dressing pad
- emergency or survival rations (alternative: energy bars)
- multifunctional tool and/or Swiss army knife
- animal repellent: (e.g. *Piexon Guardian Angel II*, *Piexon Jet Protector JPX* or pepper spray gun *Mace Pepper Gun*)
- pistol calibre 9 mm or revolver calibre .38 Special. 357 Magnum with loaded magazines/speed loaders.

For the last point it is required that you either live in a country where the possession of weapons is legal, or that your right to self-defence is more important to you than the observance of laws that criminals do not abide anyway.

6.3 Protect Yourself from Crime!

In bad economic times it is inevitable that crime will increase. Welfare benefits will lose more and more purchasing power due to inflation or even dry up completely. Not all on welfare will be able to take up normal jobs. Some will rather earn their living by robbery, theft, burglary and kidnapping. Increased immigration from regions with different moral concepts and a different attitude towards violence does not improve the situation either. As long as the criminalisation of drugs is not abolished, drug addicts can be expected to commit more and more drug-related crimes because, in hard times, people tend to escape reality by using chemical aids.

"Through my work, I have a fairly good overview, backed up by solid data, of how crime will develop, and it does not look good," says Bettina. "If the situation escalates, the police force alone will not be able to protect ordinary citizens. They will concentrate on selected officials and their own families."[8]

City residents will therefore have to get used to avoiding certain neighbourhoods, at least after dawn. Even in supposedly safe districts, it is better to walk in a group than alone because criminals like to seek out inferior victims and avoid resistance. You should protect your apartment or house more strongly against burglary, with security doors, better locks, bars, alarm systems and possibly a

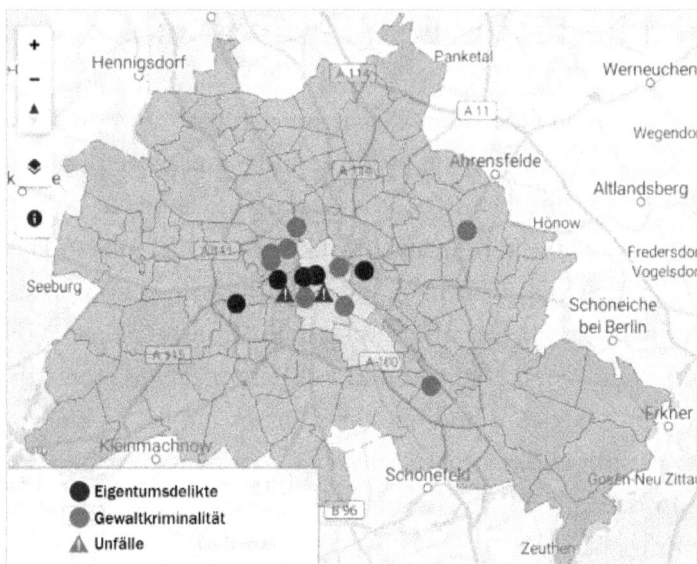

Snapshot map of crimes and accidents in Berlin

guard dog. It is likely that gated communities with private security forces and strict access control, as is common in the USA and Latin America, will also become more popular in Europe in the future, even if this makes you feel like living in a prison.

To be prepared for robberies, you should always carry a certain amount of cash with you, which you can quickly give to someone who threatens you with a gun or knife. Criminals are usually interested in closing their deals as quickly as possible. If the amount is large enough to satisfy the robber, he will most likely leave you alone and run away. Under no circumstances should you play the hero and defend your belongings, unless you are clearly superior to the robber in terms of weaponry. If he is alone and only armed with a knife that is not at your throat yet, and you can quickly pull out a gun, the situation is different. But in case of doubt you should not take any risks and write off your cash.

6.4 Strengthen your Social Network!

Humans have only been able to survive confronted with much stronger opponents such as wolves, bears or sabre-toothed tigers because they have formed groups and communicated with each other. Through life in the modern industrial society we have partially forgotten important qualities such as solidarity and mutual help. The welfare state has especially done a lot of damage here because it tries to create „solidarity" by coercion and deprives people of their own responsibility. In times of crisis we should therefore recall important qualities such as genuine solidarity, compassion and helpfulness.

"I completed a survival training course with Aborigines in the Australian desert a few years ago, which was very interesting," says Bettina Falck. "For the Aborigines, water, food, shelter and healing are of course also very important for survival, but the most important thing for them is community. We humans are not stand-alone fighters; we can only be strong in a group. This is something that many Western survivalists overlook."[9]

Social isolation, as ordered by some governments in the times of the corona panic, is exactly the wrong way to go in times of crisis. As an individual, life can be very hard in a world marked by distributional struggles and growing crime. In a community of like-minded people who stand together and support each other, things look very different. It can be your family or friends, your neighbourhood or religious community.

Bettina Falck therefore recommends, even before the crisis breaks out, to expand and strengthen your own social networks – and that doesn't mean Facebook & Co. but real networks with people of flesh and blood whom you know in person.

Mastering a major crisis will certainly not be easy, but it can also have positive aspects. The collapse of the economic and financial system will teach us to rediscover ancient human ways of living together. We will get back to this in Chapter 8. But first, let's have a look at financial freedom from a different perspective.

7. Financially Free in Mind

Perhaps you expected this book to tell you how to get rich quickly. Many books that have "Financial Freedom" in the title often talk about nothing more than achieving wealth. My interpretation of the term so far has been a different one, namely to protect your property against financial repression by the government. By financial repression I mean things like negative interest rates, capital controls, frozen bank accounts, currency reforms or hyperinflation. In chapters 2 to 6, I have described a number of measures that may serve as a defence.

But of course it is legitimate to ask where to get the money from which needs to be protected. What good is information about cryptocurrencies, gold or solid stocks if you do not have any money that you can invest in a crisis-proof way? What good are tips on states with territorial taxation where you can set up your business if you dare not found a company at all? In times of an impending crisis, it especially makes sense that you take a look at your own attitude towards money, success and wealth, because it could soon become very important for you. Perhaps your seemingly secure job will be cancelled, so you ask yourself what you should do instead. Or your successful company loses important customers and has to file for bankruptcy. You need to be mentally prepared for such critical situations.

7.1 Mind Your Mind

There are some very interesting training programmes that deal with financial freedom in a broader sense. I would like to introduce these three in the following:
- the *Millionaire's Mind* training by T. Harv Eker
- the *Wealthy Mind* training of Tim and Kris Hallbom and
- the *Diamond Cutter System* by Geshe Michael Roach.

All three see the causes of financial success as being primarily rooted in the human mind, in its unconscious attitudes and beliefs. In this chapter I can naturally only give you a first impression of these methods. If this should arouse your interest in one or more of them, I can only recommend that you do your own research. At the end of this chapter you will find more detailed information.

My Aha-Experience on Money

Personally, I had a key experience in this regard when I was in a rather poor financial position a few years ago. A friend of mine who is a coach kindly gave me a coaching for free, because I was so broke that I could not afford her sessions. I told her that money was not really important to me and that I had other goals in life than acquiring wealth. For me, money was just a "means to an end". And here she had me: "Imagine if you told your partner or friends that they were just a 'means to an end'," she said, "With an attitude like that, everyone will probably avoid your company and you will lose your partner and friends quickly. It's no different with money."

This realisation changed a lot of things in me. I realised that my distaste for money was harmful and had led to my poor financial situation. Money is nothing bad or impure, but a form of positive energy. It is an expression of other people valuing your work. I came out of this coaching purified and strengthened. In the time that followed, I built up a successful production company for internet videos and wrote several bestsellers. Today I am financially freer than ever before, although I surely have not yet fully realised my potential. The research for this chapter was a good opportunity for me to delve even deeper into the subject.

Did I already tell you how much I love my work? Making instructional videos and writing books is really awesome.

There is probably no better way to learn something yourself than to explore new topics in such depth that you can explain them to other people in simple words and pictures.

7.2 The Life Concept Ikigai

Before I go into more detail about the training methods I want to present to you, let's have a look at an interesting concept that originates from Japan, called *Ikigai*. *Iki* means life and *Gai* means value, so it is what makes life worth living and gives it value. Ikigai is the intersection of these four important aspects of life, laid out in the form of overlapping circles:

    1. what you love

    2. what you are good at

    3. what the world needs

    4. what you get paid for

For example, if your circles 1 and 2 overlap, you have found a nice hobby for yourself, but nothing more. Hardly anyone else will be interested in it. If your circles 2 and 4 overlap, you can be successful in your profession, but you will probably feel a certain senselessness. If your circles 1, 2 and 3 overlap, it can be a very fulfilling task that makes you happy, such as a volunteer position in a charitable foundation, but will not earn you a living. If you have not inherited a lot of money, you will have to complement your charitable work with a job that may only involve the inter-

1

What you love

2 What you
are good at

i

What the
world needs **3**

What you
get paid for

4

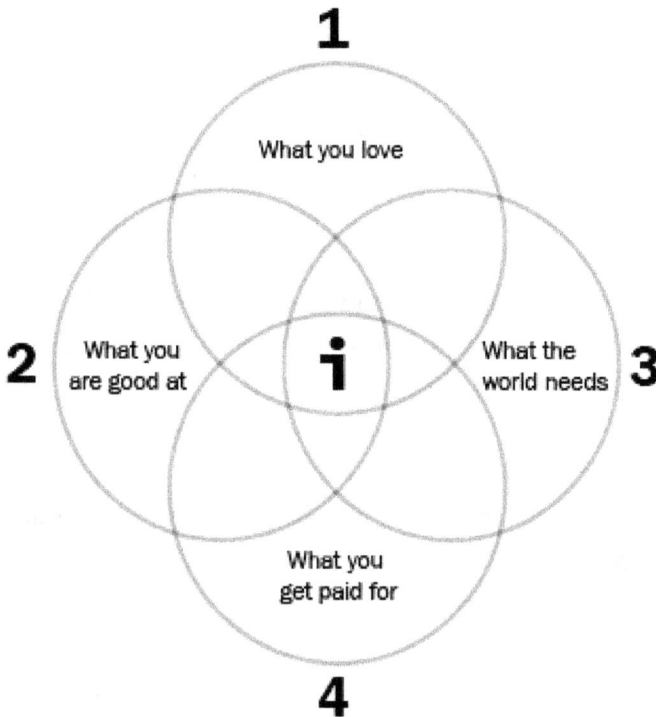

section of circles 2 and 4. So you may spend your working
hours yearning for your beautiful, fulfilling charity work.
Only when all four circles intersect is the Ikigai perfect.
Finding such a life task is not easy and may take some time.
This model can help you to become clear about what you
want to use your life for.

If you have a job that you love, in which you are really
good at, and that the world needs, there is a good chance
that you make good money with it. Nevertheless, there are
many people who, despite the best of conditions, always
have financial difficulties. What is the reason for this?

7.3 Millionaire's Mind by T. Harv Eker

T. Harv Eker, author of the book *Secrets of the Millionaire's Mind* and one of the most successful financial freedom trainers says: it is mainly due to our "financial blueprint", which most of us carry within us unconsciously. It determines our relationship to money. Often it is the result of early childhood impressions. Maybe our parents constantly said things like "Money corrupts your character" or "Rich people are greedy exploiters", and we adopt this without questioning. It may also be that earlier failures have led us to the protective assertion that money is actually not important to us at all. Instead of learning from our failures and becoming stronger, we try to downplay them and justify ourselves by saying that money and success do not really matter anyway. By this wrong attitude we attract even more failure.

T. Harv Eker hilmself has often failed in life. In 12 years, he tried to build 14 different business models, all without success. Only when a rich friend of his father's advised him to change his way of thinking and to "think like a rich man" his fortune changed. After studying the life stories and success strategies of rich people, he built up a successful chain of fitness stores and within two and a half years, sold them and became a millionaire. However, his financial happiness did not last long. Through poor financial management, his fortune shrank to almost zero. He learned painfully that it is not only important to make money, it is just as important to preserve, manage and increase your wealth wisely. It is no wonder that many lottery winners who come from poor backgrounds squander their winnings and end up as poor as before. They have never learned to handle money, and their inner financial blueprint prevents them from staying rich.

Do Not Sell Your Time!

After having lost most of his fortune, Eker delved even deeper into the subject. He developed a method for successful financial management and started his career as a coach. Today his seminars attract many people all over the world. According to his own statements, he has reached over two million people so far. He hardly ever teaches directly anymore, but has trained several coaches to teach his method. This is an important principle for becoming financially free: do not sell your own time, because it is

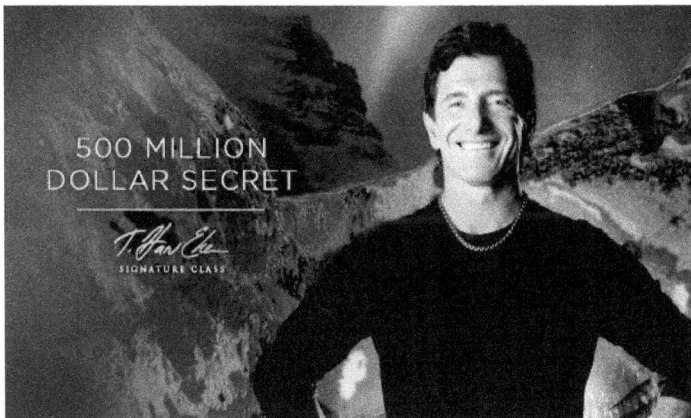

T. Harv Eker

scarce by nature, but create your own business, from which you profit most, and let other people do the operational work. Does such "unproductive income" sound immoral to you? Then you are probably broke now. Such a negative programming of the inner blueprint is the best guarantee for failure. It is only fair that T. Harv Eker benefits the most of seminars given by his certified coaches, because without his books, his videos and his blog, nobody would attend their seminars. He has built up his business in such a way that it scales well, by delegating many activities or offering courses online in the form of videos.

Even if you are still an employee, you should try not to be paid just for your time, but mainly for the results of your work, e.g. through success commissions, performance-based bonuses or stock options of the company you work for. In his book, Eker describes a meeting with a PR manager who promised to generate a media value of 20,000 US dollars per month for his company. She wanted to charge a fixed fee of 4,000 for this, but he made her the much better offer of paying 50% of the monthly media value she generated, worth 10,000 US dollars in the promised case of success. The PR manager, obviously equipped with a "poor blueprint", refused and preferred to be paid for her time, regardless of her success. Obviously, the two of them did not close a deal. If you don't take a risk and rely solely on security, you are not an adequate partner for business people who "think rich".

Focus on Passive Income!

According to Eker, the most important thing to be financially free is passive income – an income that flows even if you are not active. There are two types of passive income: one is through money that you have invested well and that you let work for you, for example in the form of shares, bonds or cryptocurrencies. The other is a business that, after investing a lot work into the startup phase, now runs by itself without you as the entrepreneur having to do much. This includes, for example, royalties from books or videos, rentals of real estate, the operation of coin-operated machines, network marketing and much more.

T. Harv Eker defines financial freedom to generate so much passive income that you can make a good living without having to work. Alternatively, if you have a modest standard and low cost of living because you emigrated to the Philippines (see Chapter 5), according to this definition you can be financially free without having to become very rich.

7.4 Wealthy Mind by Tim & Kris Hallbom

Tim and Kris Hallbom, the founders and leaders of the NLP and Coaching Centre California (NLPCA), have developed the Wealthy Mind Training. It is based on Neuro-Linguistic Programming (NLP), a system of communication techniques and methods that can change and improve psychological processes. The basic assumption is that there are connections between processes in the brain (*Neuro*), language (*Linguistic*) and habitual, unconscious behavioural patterns (*Programming*), which can be changed to achieve certain goals in life. NLP draws on a number of established forms of therapy such as Gestalt therapy and hypnotherapy, as well as findings from cognitive research.

Its founders John Grinder and Richard Bandler originally wanted to find out why some psychotherapists achieved higher healing rates than others. They studied the work of the Gestalt therapist Fritz Perls, the family therapist Virginia Satir and the hypnotherapist Milton Erikson. From these, they derived behaviours, methods and presumptions that worked particularly well in psychotherapy. Many different experts have further developed NLP. Today, it enjoys increasing popularity especially among salespeople, consultants, teachers, coaches and psychotherapists. There are numerous courses and seminars all over the world where you can be trained to become an NLP Practitioner, an NLP Master or gain other NLP-related qualifications. Critics call NLP a dubious pseudo-science, whose theses

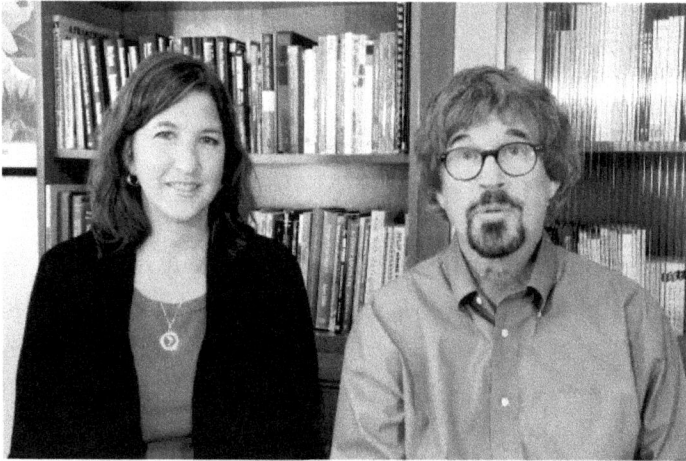
Kris and Tim Hallbom

are not proven. But this book is not about theoretical discussions, but about the very practical improvement of your own life. The best method is therefore to try out for yourself whether NLP helps you or not.

Limiting Beliefs

The Wealthy Mind programme is a two-day training that focuses on identifying and changing certain beliefs, which are preventing you from being financially successful. These are phrases like:
"You have to work hard for your money."
"It's very hard to get money."
"I'm not made to be rich."
"Money is the root of all evil."

"It is easier for a camel to go through the eye of a needle than for a rich man to enter the Kingdom of God."

Each of us has a set of beliefs about money of which we are often not aware. Nevertheless, they determine the relationship we have with money and success. If you come across "invisible ceilings" that prevent you from being financially successful, it is usually due to such negative beliefs. The Wealthy Mind training is about changing them. The training is structured as a practical workshop in small groups, in which you actively work on yourself.

Modules of the Wealthy Mind Training

1. The Universal Cycles of Change
These cycles belong to a natural process in the universe that has always existed. They can be observed in all aspects of our lives: in business, in relationships, in health, in family life and more. It is important to become aware of these cycles. People who lead successful lives are usually in harmony with them. According to the Wealthy Mind creators, how well you are in harmony with the natural cycles influences your ability to make money and achieve other positive results in life.

2. The Nine Main Attractors of Bringforthism
This funny word creation is probably supposed to trigger positive processes in the brain. What this means is the

quality of consciously deciding what you want to achieve in life, as well as developing the necessary activities to do so. Successful people are focused on these nine main attractors. The workshop is about learning how to use them.

3. Getting to Know Yourself
In this module you will examine how you unconsciously relate to money. It is about identifying the most important beliefs that limit you in terms of wealth and success.

4. Changing Our Limiting Beliefs
Our unconscious beliefs have an enormous influence on every aspect of our lives, including the financial success we can achieve. This module is about changing these limiting beliefs permanently.

5. Systemic Orientation
The final phase of the workshop is about the systemic approach, balancing your physical, mental, social, emotional and spiritual self-image with your higher goals, values, beliefs and dreams.

The basic insights of the Wealthy Mind programme are quite similar to those of T. Harv Eker, even though their methods differ significantly in style. Eker plays the shirt-sleeved American salesman with a forceful (though quite likeable) rhetoric, whereas the Hallboms come across as a bit more esoteric. With Eker you also learn practical methods to organise your finances, which is not included in the Wealthy Mind training. The NLP people claim not to limit themselves to the topic of money. They want you to experience mind in a general sense as being rich, which means open to any kind of success, be it in your love life or in society. While Eker tells his own life story (from failure to multimillionaire) to convince people, Wealthy Mind places special emphasis on its NLP basics.

7.5 The Diamond Cutter System by Geshe Michael Roach

The US American Michael Roach has a completely different background. He is a Buddhist monk and was the first Westerner to receive the title Geshe (Buddhist scholar) from Sera Monastery in Dharamsala. He became well known through his book *The Diamond Cutter – Buddhist Principles for Professional Success and Private Happiness*, which has sold millions of copies and has been translated into over 30 languages. It is based on the Buddhist Diamond Sutra[1] and derives from it how to be successful in modern business life.

In 2010 Roach founded the *Diamond Cutter Institute (DCI)*, which organises lectures and courses all over the world, either by him or by certified trainers. According to the DCI, around 30,000 people in 35 cities and 20 countries attend his courses and seminars every year.

Geshe Michael Roach

From Buddhist Monk to Businessman

After his studies at Princeton University, Roach came into contact with Tibetan Buddhism on a trip to India. After the violent annexation of Tibet by communist China in 1950, many Tibetan lamas had to flee to India. They settled mainly in the Himalayan foothills. Michael Roach met various Buddhist masters there and was fascinated by their wisdom. He became a monk himself, and after his return to the USA he lived in the monastery of his teacher Lama Sermey Khensu Lobsang Tharchin in New Jersey. After some time meditating and studying of Buddhist texts, his teacher surprised him with the task of going into the business world and practicing Buddhist teachings there.

Roach did what his master told him and found a job at the *Andin International Diamond Corporation* in New York City, which was founded in 1981 by Orthodox Jews Ofer and

173

Aya Azrielant. There he worked for about ten years, rising from apprentice to vice president. He helped to turn the small diamond cutting shop into a company with annual sales of over $250 million. In 2009, the Richline Group, owned by Warren Buffet, acquired Andin. He tells this success story in his book *The Diamond Cutter.* He parallels his experiencs to passages of the Diamond Sutra, explaining how this ancient teaching by the Buddha has helped him in his own professional life.

The Diamond Sutra

This traditional text is based on a dialogue between the Buddha and his disciple Subhuti. It was probably written down in the 1st century, after having been passed on orally since the Buddha's times. It is, by the way, the oldest printed text in the history of mankind: a wooden panel print found in 1907 is dated May 11, 868 – almost 600 years before the Gutenberg Bible.[2] The general theme of the Diamond Sutra is to see through the illusion we have of the world, which is not as real as we experience it with our senses. According to the Buddha, all things exist only in mutual interdependence. Without the observer who perceives the world, there would be no world.

This view, which is very reminiscent of modern quantum physics, is expressed by the Buddha with the words "form is emptiness – emptiness is form". The term *emptiness* does

Blockprint of the Diamond Sutra, 868 AD

not have a negative connotation in Buddhism. It means that the world does not exist by itself and is not separate from us. Therefore we can form it through our own thoughts, words and actions. We ourselves are responsible for everything that happens to us. This law of cause and effect known as *Karma* is not to be misunderstood as a fate which we have to accept. On the contrary, we can actively shape our own future Karma. Every one of our thoughts, words and actions has a direct effect on the world we will experience in the future.

175

Plant Positive Seeds in Your Mind

From this principle, Michael Roach derives the following advice, which he himself uses in his professional life:
- To prosper financially, be generous.
- To be happy, live according to ethical principles.
- To be healthy and attractive, refuse to be annoyed.
- To be a good leader, take pleasure in constructive and helpful actions
- To focus your mind, practice meditation.
- To experience the world the way you want it to, learn about the hidden potential of things.
- To get everything you want, practice compassion.

This may sound a little too abstract, and therefore Michael Roach concretely describes how to act in real-life business situations, such as:
- When your company's finances are unstable: Share your profits with those who helped you produce them.
- When your machinery is outdated or unreliable: Don't be jealous of other businessmen but focus on your own creativity and innovation.
- If you feel that you are losing your authority in the company: Don't be arrogant towards your fellow human beings; listen to those who work with you.
- If your office is full of fights and squabbles: Don't engage in conversations that aim to break people up. Ignore gossip.

Michael Roach teaches that we need to re-programme our mind. Instead of thinking about our own benefit first, we should focus on helping others. Through positive thoughts, words and actions, we plant seeds in our minds that mature over time and eventually come back to us. However, we do not think: "I am now especially nice to this person and so she will help me at some point in the future." Karma does not work like that. We say, think and do positive things without expecting anything in return. Then the positive effects will come by themselves, sometimes from a completely unexpected side.

This natural law of cause and effect can be relied upon. You just need a little patience. In the past, we have certainly planted some negative seeds that are still maturing and can lead to unpleasant experiences. It is important that we do not let ourselves be put off by them. We continue to act with loving kindness and compassion. We perceive our disturbing feelings without repressing them, yet we do not take them too seriously, so we continue to plant more and more positive seeds. Does that sound too good to be true?

Give it a try!

Web Links and Book Tips

Millionaire's Mind
www.harveker.com
T. Harv Eker: Secrets of the Millionaire Mind: Mastering the Inner Game of Wealth, Harper Business, New York 2005.

Wealthy Mind
www.thewealthymind.com
Kris and Tim Hallbom: The Magic of Bringforthism.
NLPCA San Carlos (CA), 2015.

Diamond Cutter System
www.diamondcutterinstitute.com
Geshe Michael Roach: The Diamond Cutter – The Buddha on Strategies for Managing Your Business and Your Life. Doubleday, New York, 2000

8. Imagine

It is a well know saying that in every crisis lies an opportunity. In times of crisis, old systems that seem invincible and of eternal duration may suddenly disappear. It is hard for us to imagine such dramatic changes. Just think of the "Cold War" and the division of Europe by the "Iron Curtain". Who would have imagined that in the short period from 1989 to 1991 the Berlin Wall would be torn down, all Communist regimes of Central and Eastern Europe would fall and even the highly armed superpower Soviet Union would simply dissolve?

The monetary system based on government monopolies, which today seems so normal to people that they do not even question it, can experience a similar downfall in a major crisis. And since power depends on money, the next question is whether the model of the state is not also outdated and can be replaced by better forms of organising our societies.

What Will Come After the Crisis?

Imagine that an economic and financial crisis is actually happening, a crisis more disastrous than anything the world has seen so far. National economies collapse, state structures dissolve, poverty and hunger are rampant, civil-war-like conditions prevail. Not a nice vision. But the most interesting question is: what comes next? Humans are creative beings and interested in practical solutions. We do not accept such chaotic conditions in the long run, but will look for new forms of economic and social activity that are less prone to crises. In the midst of chaos, new communities will emerge, which may have to defend themselves outside against a hostile world, but will create new forms of civilisation.

Free Competition of Cryptocurrencies

Imagine that the old monetary system has imploded. In the newly emerging islands of civilisation everyone uses cryptocurrencies because they have proven to be solid and crisis-proof. Some of the remaining central banks try to issue their own pseudo-"cryptocurrencies", but no-body wants them. People do not trust the banks or central banks anymore. Their memory of the great crisis is too vivid for that. Moreover, banks and central banks have become obsolete.

All the cryptocurrencies in use are completely decentral-ised, without any central power and middlemen. Some of the early cryptocoins like Bitcoin still play a role, but new ones have appeared, which are even faster, safer and more anonymous. No one is forced to use any particular type of money. There is no "legal tender". The decision for or against a currency is absolutely voluntary.

Voluntary Payments Instead of Taxes

This principle of voluntariness now applies in all areas of life. Taxes are no longer rounded up because it has been proven time and again that a tax regime invites abuse and waste by the powerful elites. Instead, community tasks are financed by transparent fees, which may only be used for the purpose for which they are levied.

Some communities even use money as a democratic in-strument. Each project under discussion is given its own Bitcoin address (or the address of its preferred cryptocur-rency). There may be one address for the public swim-ming pool, one for the public library, one for the public transportation system, etc. Citizens can pool money into the addresses of projects they consider worthy of funding and, if not enough money is collected to realise a project, it is cancelled and the deposits are automatically returned to the contributors. Similar to the process known from crowd funding platforms like Kickstarter or Indiegogo, this ensures only those community projects that the citizens really want and consider useful are implemented. The original budget cannot be overrun. There is no money available beyond the amount paid in.

Free Private Cities

Free private cities as conceived by Titus Gebel and others (see Chapter 5.3) have become very popular. They are operated by private, profit-oriented companies. These operating companies offer services that are essential for human coexistence, such as security and jurisdiction. Other specialised companies compete with each other to provide civic services like road construction, education, health insurance or social security. They charge a clearly defined fee for their services and guarantee delivery as promised. Organising these things in a market-based competition turned out to be much more economical and efficient.

The companies which operate the cities are also in fierce competition with each other. They must offer the highest possible quality of life at the lowest possible price, otherwise customers will decide to move to another city. Free private cities are not governed democratically but managed as a business.

Theoretically, the operating companies could operate dictatorially, just like an operator of a cruise ship or a shopping centre could, but in practice would never do. They wouls always put the needs of their customers first, as this is the only way to survive in competition. Voting is not done by ballot paper, but by feet − or rather by wallet.

There are some private cities that only accept members of certain religions, ethnic groups or sexual minorities, but most cities are open to everyone. One project was set up with the intention of finally implementing real Socialism -- with socialised means of production, everyone receiving the same salary, and no private property. However, this city was never built due to lack of customer interest...

Bottom-Up Democracy

In addition to the free private cities, people also live in other self-organised communities, especially in already populated areas that could not simply be handed over to a private operator. Here a new form of democracy has established itself, which does not have the weaknesses of the old model. In the past, power lay with parties and oligarchies, and elections did not change that. The Buddhist master Shamar Rinpoche developed the new model of a Bottom-up Democracy. He lived as a Tibetan refugee in India and observed that the supposedly "largest democracy in the world" was in reality dominated by corrupt party oligarchies. Votes were either bought with bribes or won through populist measures that were harmful to the overall system.

In his book *Creating a Transparent Democracy*,[1] Shamar Rinpoche proposes a system that works entirely without parties. It is consistently built from the bottom up. Citizens elect their representatives to the parliament of their village or neighbourhood. Here they know which problems need to be solved and whom they trust most to do that. The local parliamentarians are under constant observation of their voters and are only re-elected if they do a good job. The local parliament sends a delegate to the parliament of the next higher level, such as the city or district. This delegate can be recalled at any time, so he must act in the interest of his constituency. This parliament then sends delegates to the next encompassing tier, e.g. the province, which then sends delegates to the state, and so forth.

Small Units Replace Big Empires

Shamar Rinpoche has originally developed this model for India and therefore proposed further levels up to the federal parliament in Delhi. But after the crisis, there are no states as large as India. After all the experiences of the past, smaller units have proven to be much better suited to organise the coexistence of people.[2] In terms of population, most of the new communities range between Liechtenstein (just under 40,000) and Luxembourg (around 600,000), few are as large as Estonia (around 1.3 million).

Thus, the distances between the directly elected local parliaments and the higher levels consisting of delegates are never too big. The formation of oligarchies which are only interested in retaining their own power is closely watched and, if necessary, nipped in the bud. The crisis has made people very sensitive to this. Parliaments may only decide on things that really matter for the whole community. They do not interfere in the daily life of the citizens or in the economy.

Through the Internet, those many thousands of small communities that now exist on earth can join together at any time to form alliances, for example for defence or trade. The model for this is the *Hanseatic League*, a powerful confederation of cities that dominated trade on the Baltic Sea from the 12th to the 17th century, without a centre of power or a government authority. Today, Blockchain technology makes it possible to build a consensus between many thousands of small units who, like Bitcoin miners, do not know or trust each other. Blockchain technology is also used for elections and referendums, so that they are guaranteed to be forgery-proof and secret. All decisions of local parliaments are stored in the Blockchain in a public and immutable manner. They can be checked by the citizens at any time, but may not be changed arbitrarily.

Communities Replace the Welfare State

People are much more mobile than before. They move from one private city to the next or try out one of the many democratically organised communities. Immigration is not seen as a problem anymore, because there is no longer a welfare system which could be abused by immigrants who would live at the expense of the original inhabitants. Those who move to a new area have to earn thei onw money or rely on their family or other social networks. Borders are therefore much more open than in the days of nation states. Only those who do not follow the rules or harm other people are expelled.

Since a welfare state no longer exists, people have to cooperate with each other again. Families, friendships, neighbourhoods and religious communities have become much more important. Friendly societies and other cooperative forms of mutual insurance are once again enjoying great popularity. In the 19th century, these voluntary organisations were very successful, especially in the labour movement. They provided their members with inexpensive insurance against illness, unemployment and other risks. First in Germany, then in England and other countries, they were robbed of their basis by compulsory state insurance. The German Chancellor Otto von Bismarck, who hated the labour movement, introduced compulsory insurance to weaken it in favour of state power.[3]

The return to voluntary forms of organisation has changed the way people behave towards each other. Genuine solidarity is back in high gear. Egoists and sociopaths are frowned upon. Geshe Michael Roach's way of thinking – to always focus on helping others first – has become the general standard, not just among Buddhists.

Is all this too utopian for you? If I had predicted in 1988 that the Berlin Wall would fall the next year and that the Soviet Union would no longer exist in three years, you would have declared me crazy too. Crises make many things possible that were previously thought impossible.

I deliberately gave this last chapter the title of the well-known song by John Lennon, so that I can finally claim:

"You may say that I'm a dreamer, but I'm not the only one." [4]

Acknowledgements

I thank my experts Steffen Krug, Christoph Heuermann and Bettina Falck, without whom a large part of this book would not exist.

Thanks to Yacine Teraï for funding the English translation, which was made by Adrian Sanders and improved by George Burke – thanks to both for the great job!

I would also like to thank Prof. Thorsten Polleit for his advice on all economic issues and Jeff Gallas for his feedback on crypto currencies and the Lightning Network. Thanks also to Angela Bachfeld, Boris Adloff, and Torsten Sewing for their support.

Thanks to Gabriel Barranco for the cover photo, Denise Valois for the photo assistance and Joe Diaz of Tierra Huichol for the skull consultation.

Comments

1. Is a Crash Inevitable?

1 Marc Friedrich, Matthias Welt: Weltsystem-Crash Finanzbuchverlag München, 2019

2 Max Otte: Der größte Crash aller Zeiten, Eichborn, Frankfurt/Main, 2019

3 Dirk Müller: Machtbeben – Die Welt vor der größten Wirtschaftskrise aller Zeiten, Heyne, München, 2018

4 https://www.dbresearch.com/PROD/RPS_EN -PROD/ PROD0000000000503196/Imagine_2030.PDF

5 Charlie Shrem: A Geek in Prison — Part 13 — MackerelCoin & My Socioeconomic Observations of Prison https://medium.com/@cshrem/a-geek-in-prison-part-13-mackerel-coin-my-socioeconomic-observations-of-prisonebc057a83e1d

6 Karl Marx, Friedrich Engels: Das Kommunistische Manifest, Create Space, 2017. https://www.amazon.de/Daskommunistische-Manifest-Karl-Marx/dp/1973968800/

7 Friedrich August von Hayek: The Denationalisation of Money, Institute of Econmic Affairs, London, 1976.

8 Dirk Müller: Machtbeben – die Welt vor der größten Wirtschaftskrise aller Zeiten. S. 193 Heyne, München, 2018.

9 https://www.welt.de/vermischtes/article106186204/Nie-mand-will-in-Chinas-riesiger-Geisterstadt-leben.html

10 https://commodity.com/debt-clock/japan/

11 https://supchina.com/2020/04/09/more-than-240000-chinese-compa-nies-declare-bankruptcy-in-the-first-two-months-of-2020/

12 https://www.bloomberg.com/graphics/2018-lehman-debt/

13 https://fortune.com/2016/06/10/bill-gross-supernova-negative-inter-est-rates/

14 Johannes Eisleben: Corona könnte den Schuldenturm kippen. Achse des Guten, März 2020: https://www.achgut.com/artikel corona_koennte_den_ schuldenturm_kippen

15 https://www.misesde.org/?p=22354

16 https://www.misesde.org/?p=22792

17 https://www.finanzen100.de/finanznachrichten/boerse/es-geht-mit-riesenschritten-voran-bis-zur-naechsten-krise-istdas-bargeld-abgeschafft_H32258001_11431485/?fbclid=IwAR1eASklZ_V6zRuQ9u4YoqZxM-HeknnGT9f2gGXwXyB4jEjb8v3FQvunj1oI

18 https://www.ecb.europa.eu/press/pr/date/2020/html/ecb.pr200318_1~3949d6f266.en.html

19 https://www.ft.com/content/9575e856-6ed3-11ea-9bca-bf503995cd6f

2. Digital Cash

1 https://Bitcoin.org/Bitcoin.pdf

2 https://www.nasdaq.com/articles/genesis-files-how-david-chaums-ecash-spawned-cypherpunk-dream-2018-04-24

3 https://en.Bitcoin.it/wiki/Hashcash

4 https://en.Bitcoin.it/wiki/B-money

5 https://www.investopedia.com/terms/b/bit-gold.asp

6 The contents of the block are encrypted with a method called Hashing. Its output always has the same size, regardless of its input. The data in the block is then combined with a random number called nonce to produce different results. The miner now calculates different hashes until it finds one that is less than a certain value, which means it begins with a certain amount of zeros. This maximum size is reset every two weeks. You have to calculate many different hashes until you find one that meets the criteria.

7 A halving takes place every 210,000 blocks, so the exact time between the halving dates depends on how much time is needed to find the blocks.

8 The public key is processed to generate a Bitcoin address. It is supplemented by an identification number and a check digit. The identification number indicates that it is a Bitcoin address. The check digit can be used to catch typing errors.

9 A good overview of the most important wallets can be found at https://Bitcoin.org/en/choose-your-wallet.

10 MtGo steht für das Fantasy-Spiel Magic: the Gathering Online, X für Exchange.

3. Is Bitcoin Crisis-Proof?

1 https://Bitcointalk.org/index.php?topic=137.0

2 Peter Kugler and Peter Bernholz: The Price Revolution in the 16th Century: Empirical Results from a Structural Vectorautoregression Model, University of Basel, 2007 https://www.econstor.eu/bitstream/10419/123383/1/wp2007-12.pdf

3 https://www.goldindustrygroup.com.au/news/2016/7/7/gold-investor-series-stock-to-flow-why-gold-is-not-acommodity

4 https://www.lookintoBitcoin.com/charts/stock-to-flow-model/

5 In this calculation we neglect the fact that of the theoretically existing Bitcoins, several million are probably lost due to forgotten passwords and carelessly thrown away hard disks. Bitcoin is therefore even scarcer than originally planned.

7 https://news.Bitcoin.com/no-internet-no-problem-how-to-send-bitcon-by-amateur-radio/?fbclid=IwAR0RCQNTjZ-os7a5rA0ek7Y4D8WhywsthhiverQBf8uVx5ecE1BGf3c_0lg

8 https://blockstream.com/2019/05/11/en-gotenna-satellite-api-integration/

9 https://www.Bitcoinmarketjournal.com/how-many-people-use-Bitcoin/

10 https://www.bloomberg.com/news/articles/2018-01-30/crypto-exchange-bitfinex-tether-said-to-get-subpoenaed-bycftc

4. Austrian Investing

1 Ludwig v. Mises: *Human Action – A Treatise on Economics*, Yale University Press, New York, 1949.

2 https://www.facebook.com/photo.php?fbid=10221441039436367&-set=a.10200332391813369&type=3&theater

3 Murray Rothbard: *America's Great Depression*, Van Nostrand, NYC, 1963.

4 Ludwig v. Mises: *Human Action – A Treatise on Economics*, Yale University Press, New York, 1949.

5 Interview with the author, January 2020

6 Interview with the author, January 2020

7 Interview with the author, January 2020

8 Prof. Thorsten Polleit: Bitcoin, Hoffnungsträger für besseres Geld https://www.misesde.org/2013/12/Bitcoinhoffnungstrager-fur-besseres-geld/

9 Rahim Taghizagedan, Ronald Stöfele, Mark Valek: Österreichische Schule für Anleger, Seiten 223-224. Finanzbuchverlag München, 2014.

10 Rahim Taghizagedan, Ronald Stöfele, Mark Valek: Österreichische Schule für Anleger, Seiten 224-225. Finanzbuchverlag München, 2014.

5. Get Out of Tax Hell

1 Found on Christoph Heuermanns Facebook-Profil: https://www.facebook.com/christoph.heuermann

2 https://www.prosieben.de/tv/galileo/videos/2017147-leben-ohne-steuern-wie-geht-das-clip

3 Ludwig Erhard: Über den "Lebensstandard", Die Zeit, Hamburg, 15.8.1958. https://www.zeit.de/1958/33/ueberden-lebensstandard/komplettansicht

4 To which Friedrich August von Hayek dedicated his book "The Road to Serfdom", 1944 University of Chicago Press, Chicago.

5 Roland Baader: Ein Staatsbegräbnis für Freiheit und Wohlstand in: Kompass – Streitschrift für Politik und Medien, Ausgabe 3 / 2003.
6 https://www.theeuropean.de/juergen-fritz/12710-weniger-als-ein-drittel-sind-nettosteuerzahler

7 https://www.insm.de/insm/presse/pressemeldungen/emnid-umfrage-spitzensteuersatz-einkommensgrenze

8 https://de.statista.com/statistik/daten/studie/2534/umfrage/entwicklung-der-anzahl-deutscher-auswanderer/

9 https://www.staatenlos.ch/flaggentheorie-2/

10 The flag theory was made known to a wider audience through these two books: W.G. Hill: *PT: A coherent plan for a stress-free, healthy and prosperous life without government interference, taxes or coercion"*, Scope International Ltd. *Waterlooville 1989* and W.G. Hill: *PT2: The practice: freedom and privacy tactics: A reference handbook*, Scope International Ltd. Waterlooville 1993. W.G. Hill is probably a pseudonym; according to the publisher, the books are "inspired and edited by Harry D.Schultz."

11 Harry D. Schultz: How to Keep Your Money and Your Freedom, Exodus, NYC, 1975.

12 https://www.staatenlos.ch/panama-wohnsitz/

13 https://www.staatenlos.ch/das-beste-ziel-zum-auswandern-nach-asien/

14 https://www.staatenlos.ch/wohnsitz-paraguay/
15 https://www.staatenlos.ch/georgien/

16 Titus Gebel: "Free Private Cities – Make Governments Compete for You", Aquila Urbis Verlag, Walldorf, 2018

17 Interview with the author, January 2020

18 https://www.bundestag.de/parlament/geschichte/gastredner/benedict/rede-250244

6. Mastering the Crisis

1 Interview with the author, January 2020

2 Interview with the author, January 2020

3 Lecture by Andreas Antonpoulus on privacy at the Latin American Bitcoin Conference Montevideo, 13 December 2019.

4 The title of the chapter on anonymity in Bettina Falck's book, freely adapted from René Descartes.

5 Lecture by Andreas Antonpoulus on privacy at the Latin American Bitcoin Conference Montevideo, 13 December 2019.

6 https://www.bbk.bund.de/SharedDocs/Downloads/BBK/DE/Publikationen/Broschueren_Flyer/Buergerinformationen_A4/Ratgeber_Brosch.pdf?__blob=publicationFile

7 Interview with the author, January 2020

8 Interview with the author, January 2020

9 Interview with the author, January 2020

7. Financially Free in Mind

1 Sanskrit: Vajracchedikā-prajñāpāramitā-Vajracchedikā

2 Johann Gutenberg did not invent printing itself, but printng with movable type, which is much faster and more efficient than other techniques.

8. Imagine

1 Shamar Rinpoche: Creating a Transparent Democracy – A New Model. Bird of Paradise Press, Delhi, 2015.

2 https://mises.org/wire/small-countries-are-better-theyre-often-richer-and-safer-big-countries

3 https://www.fuw.ch/article/bismarck-mein-gedanke-war-die-arbei-tenden-klassen-zu-gewinnen/

4 John Lennon: *Imagine*, from the album with the same title, Apple Records, 1971.

Images

Page 5 Rodolfo Andragnes

Page 12 Shutterstock 148925300

Page 13 http://wirtschaftlichefreiheit.de/
wordpress/?p=23463

Page 14 Trading Economics / European Central Bank

Page 18 WikiCommons

Page 23 Trading Economics / European Central Bank

Page 27 Enrique López Garre / Pixabay

Page 28 Shutterstock 375755044

Page 35 Trading Economics / European Central Bank

Page 41 Aaron Koenig

Page 44 Gerd Altmann / Pixabay

Page 47 Max Cryptohead / 21heads.com

Page 50 Coinmarketcap.com

Page 55 Satoshi Labs

Page 56 Satoshi Labs Acinq

Page 69 Satoshi Labs

Page 73 Shutterstock 784917253

Page 75 Laszlo Hanyecz / Bitcointalk.org

Page 78 Pixabay

Page 79 LookintoBitcoin.com

Page 88 Coinmarketcap

Page 91 Money on Chain

Page 95 CC by Dr. Bernd Gross

Page 97 Creative Commons (§7 Österreichisches
Urhebergesetz)

Page 99 CC by Ludwig von Mises Institute

Page 103 Steffen Krug

Page 105 Aaron Koenig

Page 113 Shutterstock 648072241

Page 114 Christoph Heuermann

Page 119 Aaron Koenig / NASA

Page 125 Wiki Commons

Page 127 Wiki Commons

Page 129 Wiki Commons

Page 131 Wiki Commons

Page 133 Aaron Koenig / Google Maps

Page 140 Shutterstock 412463713

Page 142 Bettina Falck

Page 154 Bettina Falck

Page 158 Shutterstock 706101307

Page 162 Aaron Koenig

Page 163 T. Harv Eker

Page 167 NLPCA

Page 172 CC 4.0 by Helene Sh WikiCommons

Page 173 WikiCommons

Page 178 Shutterstock 503106388

Do You Want to Know More About Bitcoin and Austrian Economics?

21HEADS

Portraits of Crypto Pioneers
by Max Cryptohead

21heads.com